Viking Myths, Legends and History

An Enthralling Exploration of Norse Mythology, Stories of Norsemen, and Vikings in England

© Copyright 2024 - All rights reserved.

The content contained within this book may not be reproduced, duplicated, or transmitted without direct written permission from the author or the publisher.

Under no circumstances will any blame or legal responsibility be held against the publisher, or author, for any damages, reparation, or monetary loss due to the information contained within this book, either directly or indirectly.

Legal Notice:

This book is copyright protected. It is only for personal use. You cannot amend, distribute, sell, use, quote, or paraphrase any part, or the content within this book, without the consent of the author or publisher.

Disclaimer Notice:

Please note the information contained within this document is for educational and entertainment purposes only. All effort has been executed to present accurate, up-to-date, reliable, and complete information. No warranties of any kind are declared or implied. Readers acknowledge that the author is not engaging in the rendering of legal, financial, medical, or professional advice. The content within this book has been derived from various sources. Please consult a licensed professional before attempting any techniques outlined in this book.

By reading this document, the reader agrees that under no circumstances is the author responsible for any losses, direct or indirect, that are incurred as a result of the use of the information contained within this document, including, but not limited to, errors, omissions, or inaccuracies.

Free limited time bonus

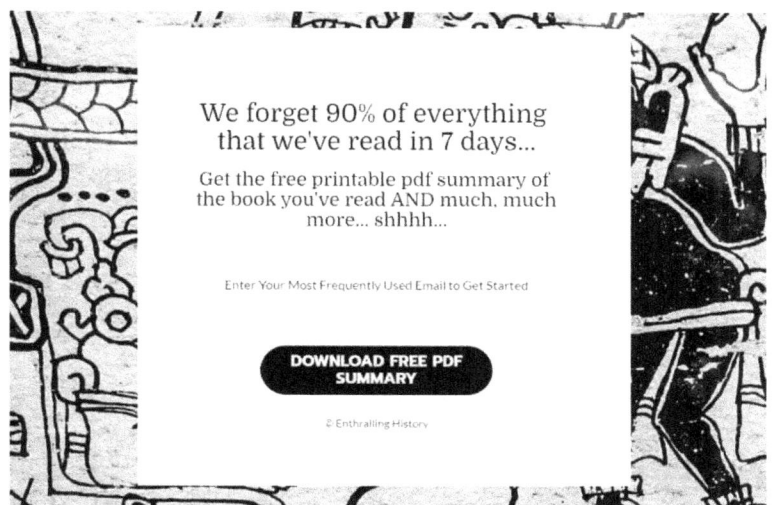

Stop for a moment. We have a free bonus set up for you. The problem is this: we forget 90% of everything that we read after 7 days. Crazy fact, right? Here's the solution: we've created a printable, 1-page pdf summary for this book that you're reading now. All you have to do to get your free pdf summary is to go to the following website:

https://livetolearn.lpages.co/enthrallinghistory/

Or, Scan the QR code!

Once you do, it will be intuitive. Enjoy, and thank you!

Table of Contents

PART 1: VIKING MYTHS AND LEGENDS 1
    INTRODUCTION 2
    CHAPTER ONE: AN INTRODUCTION TO VIKING HISTORY................. 3
    CHAPTER TWO: A VIKING LEGEND: GRETTIR THE OUTLAW 12
    CHAPTER THREE: A GUIDE TO NORSE DEITIES 19
    CHAPTER FOUR: THE NORSE COSMOS: THE DAWN OF TIME........... 28
    CHAPTER FIVE: YGGDRASIL AND THE NINE REALMS......................... 35
    CHAPTER SIX: ODIN THE ALL-FATHER 43
    CHAPTER SEVEN: VALHALLA AND THE AFTERLIFE............................. 49
    CHAPTER EIGHT: FREYJA, THE GODDESS FOR ALL SEASONS 56
    CHAPTER NINE: THOR, GOD OF THUNDER... 60
    CHAPTER TEN: LEGENDARY CREATURES FROM NORSE MYTHS 67
    CHAPTER ELEVEN: LOKI, THE TRICKSTER GOD, AND THE
    BEGINNING OF THE END... 73
    CHAPTER TWELVE: RAGNARÖK, TWILIGHT OF THE GODS 81
    CONCLUSION 86
PART 2: VIKINGS IN ENGLAND... 89
    INTRODUCTION 90
    CHAPTER ONE: THE FIRST VIKING RAIDS (780–850 CE)..................... 92
    CHAPTER TWO: RAGNAR LOTHBROK... 104
    CHAPTER THREE: THE GREAT HEATHEN ARMY 112
    CHAPTER FOUR: ALFRED THE GREAT 123
    CHAPTER FIVE: THE DANELAW 131

CHAPTER SIX: EDWARD AND ÆTHELSTAN 140
CHAPTER SEVEN: SWEYN FORKBEARD AND CNUT THE GREAT 154
CHAPTER EIGHT: STAMFORD BRIDGE AND HASTINGS....................... 165
CHAPTER NINE: LIFE OF A VIKING IN ENGLAND................................. 175
CONCLUSION.. 183
HERE'S ANOTHER BOOK BY ENTHRALLING HISTORY THAT YOU MIGHT LIKE.. 186
FREE LIMITED TIME BONUS 187
BIBLIOGRAPHY... 188

Part 1: Viking Myths and Legends

Enthralling Tales, Stories, and History of the Vikings and Norse Mythology

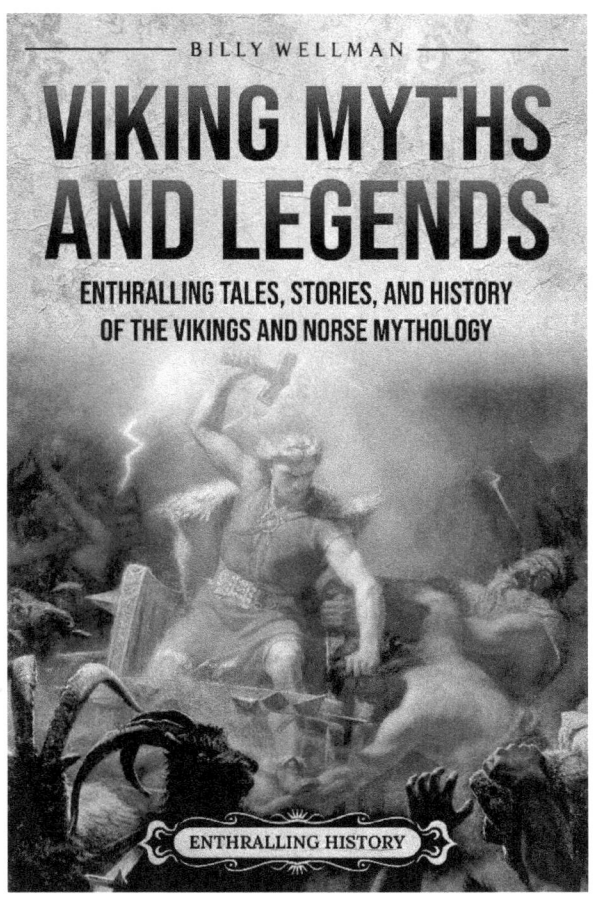

Introduction

Viking myths have captivated audiences for centuries. Eagerly awaited blockbusters, video games, books, and comics have made some of these figures common household names and even Halloween costumes.

But is there more to these Viking gods than is often depicted? This book dives into the stories and myths that are well loved and explores some of the legends that may not be as well known. See why Thor dressed as a goddess and why Loki birthed a horse. How did the Vikings believe the world began? And how did they think it ended?

This book goes beyond just the myths and talks about how Christianity impacted the telling of these legendary sagas. Discover how Viking history interweaves with their stories and why myths and legends are so important to learn about today.

There is so much to unpack in this book. We hope you enjoy this ride through fantasy and history!

Chapter One: An Introduction to Viking History

In 793 CE, medieval Christians in Europe were shocked and appalled at an audacious attack on the peaceful monastery on the holy island of Lindisfarne. It was a vicious raid. The church, according to the scholar Alcuin's letters, was "spattered with blood of the priests of God, despoiled of all its ornaments," after which the strangers, regardless of the carnage they had wreaked on one of the most sacred sites of Christendom in Europe, "trampled on the bodies of saints in the temple of God, like dung in the street." Another chronicler, the monk Symeon of Durham Priory, wrote (albeit some two hundred years later) that they "laid everything waste with grievous plundering, trampled the holy places with polluted steps, dug up the altars and seized all the sea."[1]

The Domesday Stone, a 9th-century grave marker at the priory, depicts a line of seven warriors with their weapons held aloft, preparing for attack. The stone is thought to commemorate this event, which would not be an isolated attack. It was the start of what has become known as the Viking Age.

The Lindisfarne Monastery had been established in the previous century by Irish monk and missionary Aidan, the "Apostle of Northumbria." It held the holy relics of Saint Cuthbert, who legendarily

---

[1] *Volume 2 of Symeonis monachi Opera omnia.* Symeon of Durham. Edited by Thomas Arnold. Oxford University Press, 1965.

healed the sick and expelled several demons from northern England. Pilgrims thronged to his shrine, hoping for miracles or enlightenment. As it became an established center of the Christian faith, kings, nobles, and commoners showered it with gifts of lands, treasures, and other valuables, each hoping to buy salvation.

This holy site could not have been a better target for the three or four ships of the Scandinavian raiders determined to snatch enough silver to buy them land, status, and brides back home. At the priory, there was a whole host of gleaming prizes ripe for the picking and all under one roof. These treasures were barely defended by holy men who had no chance of making any sort of stand against such an onslaught.

As it was recorded in the *Anglo-Saxon Chronicle*, the Vikings robbed and slaughtered without any care for religious sentiment. The raiders crammed their ships with treasure and enslaved monks before setting sail for home, most likely Norway. The people left behind in the church were left wringing their hands in anguish. Christian scholars concluded that it could only be the sinfulness of the people of Northumbria that had left God reluctant to protect the monastery and the holy island.

The Lindisfarne attack was not the first Viking raid. They had already ransacked a Northumbrian monastery at Jarrow, and there had been several attacks in southern England. In 788, three longships landed at Portland. Once ashore, the Vikings slew the reeve of Dorchester, who had ill-advisedly approached them to try and find out the purpose of their arrival and had attempted to take them to the royal manor, according to the *Anglo-Saxon Chronicle*.

The early years of the Viking Age continued in the same vein. In 795, Viking raiders made their first attack on Iona Abbey in the Scottish Hebrides and then made three more raids on that same island in the decade that followed. In 806, the Vikings massacred sixty-eight monks in what has become known as Martyr's Bay. Afterward, many of the Iona survivors fled to the Abbey of Kells in Ireland, which almost certainly saved their lives since the Vikings returned in 825 to burn down the abbey. They killed the rest of the monks who remained.

Vikings came from what is now Norway, Sweden, and Denmark. In the early part of the Viking Age, it was primarily Norwegian raiders responsible for the attacks on Britain and Ireland. The Danes and Swedes tended to wreak havoc on mainland Europe.

The people of these countries were not all known as Vikings. The name has come to define a particular section of the Norse communities: medieval Scandinavian seafarers who were accomplished sailors and adventurers, violent pirates and thieves, and ruthless slave traders.

In Norse society, thralls, or enslaved people, were the lowest class. The Vikings' prisoners of war were often enslaved, and some armed raiders set out on specific slaving missions, sailing from coast to coast in northwestern Europe in search of peaceful communities where young men and women could be taken. There were violent abductions, and some victims were restrained (medieval iron shackles have been unearthed at Viking trading posts at Birka in Sweden and Hedeby in Denmark). The undoubtedly traumatized people who had been kidnapped and taken far from their native lands often passed through several hands, having been bought and then sold at slave markets or to the Anglo-Saxon nobility. Few remained in Scandinavia. After the raid on the priory at Lindisfarne, Alcuin tried to raise funds for the release of the monks that the Vikings had taken.

Although Vikings risked their lives on the treacherous northern seas, most Norsemen quietly farmed their land. They grew crops such as barley, oats, rye, and peas and reared pigs, goats, cattle, and horses to provide enough food for their families and sometimes their extended families. However, the soil was poor, and the benefits of fertilizer had not yet been understood by the Norse farmers in the Middle Ages. The tradition was for the oldest son to inherit the farm, so younger sons generally found themselves having to make their own way in the world. The lure of adventure and comradeship, plus the opportunity to acquire enough silver to buy their own land, must have been a tempting and heady proposition for those young men.

It was a hard life for the Norse in Scandinavia during the Middle Ages for those who were not landowners. The cold climate presented its own difficulties with bitter, freezing winters, and there were periodic shortages of herring, which was a main food source for the population. Paradoxically, in some years, there was a surplus of food to take abroad and trade alongside their usual cargoes of furs, iron, timber, and amber, which they exchanged for gold, silver, silks, and spices from southern traders.

As other nations ramped up their overseas trading, there was always the possibility for the Vikings to indulge in a bit of piracy. As the Viking Age developed, there was even the possibility of settling overseas in Britain,

Ireland, mainland Europe, or even in the small colonies the Vikings established in the faraway lands of Iceland, Greenland, and North America.

Scandinavia was an ideal place to set out to sea and explore the lands to the west. Skilled Norse shipbuilders developed techniques of building strong and fast longships by overlapping planks of ash wood over a ribbed frame that was riveted together with iron pins. Longships made for raiding were symmetrical so that the crew could reverse direction without having to turn the craft around. These ships accommodated a crew of twenty-five to thirty people.

Knarr ships, which were used for trading, were much larger (around sixteen meters or fifty-two feet) and deeper and broader (around five meters or sixteen feet) than the traditional longships. They could carry some twenty-four tons of cargo and a crew of sixty. The knarr ships were not just robust and swift; they were also light enough to be carried or dragged on shore. It was in these knarr ships that Vikings navigated the Atlantic Ocean. Only one of these larger ships has ever been found. It was discovered in the Roskilde Fjord in Denmark; it is now carefully preserved in the local museum.

When the Vikings returned to their homes and hung up their axes, they toiled the soil or worked as craftsmen (such as blacksmiths or shipbuilders), traders, or fishermen. Raids were generally conducted during the summer months when the seas tended to be calmer. That way, the Vikings could return to help with the autumn harvests. Eventually, raiding unprotected, wealthy monasteries became so profitable and lucrative that they found they had no real need to do anything else.

Young men and women were considered to have reached maturity by the age of twelve. Boys at that age were working as adults, managing their lands or working as blacksmiths, sailors, or craftsmen. By the age of twenty, most were married and had become parents.

It is worth noting that women married to Viking farmers were generally considered capable of managing the land in their partner's absence. Women were respected. Female physical abuse was condemned as shameful, and women had better rights than in many contemporary European cultures. For instance, they were able to divorce if they had reason and own property. Although most women were responsible for the homesteads, it is likely that a few had roles in trade and as warriors since scales and weapons have been discovered in excavated graves of females.

The pagan Norse religion and beliefs had been practiced since before 500 BCE. It was polytheistic, meaning there were several deities, both male and female. Worshiping was closely associated with the seasons and the cycles of the year. It was usual for worshipers to congregate in the open air or at natural landmarks. The sacred spaces around these sacred groves, streams, mountains, rocks, or trees were marked by stone or branch boundaries. It is widely believed worshipers left offerings and performed rituals in the hope of ensuring fertility, prosperity, and safety as a part of their daily lives. However, in the remains of multifunctional complexes that include mead halls for public festivals, fenced areas containing a *hörgr* (a kind of altar often consisting of a pile of stones) have been discovered. Some prominent sites can be found on the Lofoten Islands in Norway and Funen in Denmark.

The German medieval chronicler Adam of Bremen wrote an account of the pagan rituals that were performed in Gamla Uppsala in Sweden. He described a temple (*hof*) that was gilded inside and contained three statues of Norse gods. Thor, one of the most important gods, was placed in the center. He ruled the skies and held a scepter. It was hoped that Thor would provide mild weather for farmers and sailors. Odin was represented as a warrior. He was the god of war and victory, whereas "Fricco" (or Freyr) was the god of peace and fertility. Each of these gods had his own priest, and according to Adam, a great festival was held at the temple every nine years. People from all over Scandinavia traveled to attend it.

Human sacrifices did occur. More than seventy-two corpses were left hanging in the surrounding trees, and there was a building dedicated to libation rituals (the pouring of liquid or grains as an offering). The remains of the Gamla Uppsala *hof* have been excavated. The longhouse was more than one hundred meters (over three hundred feet) in length and originally dated to between 600 and 800 CE.

This festival was likely what is known as the *blót* in Old Norse, a common feast that was held for nine days every nine years in Scandinavian and Germanic countries. At Swedish pagan *blót* ceremonies, nine males of each animal species would be sacrificed, including humans.

Although there was no apparent faith leader like in most communities, several Nordic runestones refer to people bearing the title *gothi* in early medieval Nordic villages, especially in Iceland, which the Vikings settled in the late 800s CE. It is possible these officials had a religious standing, but it is more likely they were respected senior figures responsible for political issues, law and order, and matters of faith. The sagas refer to seeresses called *völva* and wise male elders called *thul* who are thought to have been involved in the praising of Norse gods through reciting poetry and singing.

Marriages were a cause of great celebration in pagan Scandinavia. Families found brides for their sons. Once the new couple's inheritance and the bride's dowry had been negotiated, the betrothal was sealed with a gift from the young man's parents. The two families were then bound together, and the contract was sealed at the wedding, which was a public ceremony and feast that often lasted several days.

Birthing a baby was a perilous time for medieval mothers and babies. Norse myths, legends, and sagas give a good understanding of the cultural practices of the time. Expectant mothers sang and performed rituals to the maternal goddesses, such as Frigg and Freyja, for the safe delivery of their children and for a favorable moment for their births. As these deities were thought to be present during childbirth, this natural process was accepted as a part of family and society (unlike some other cultures that considered it an offensive and unclean time).

Nine nights after the baby's delivery, the child was taken to the head of the family, who would sit it on his knee and sprinkle water over it–very much like a baptism. It is possible that the wider family was present and would bring gifts.

After this ceremony, the baby was considered a full member of the clan. If it were to be killed by its parents, they would be considered guilty of murder. (Newborns were, on occasion, killed within their first nine days if it was thought they would not survive.)

Vikings had a strong belief in predestined fate. They chose their ancestors or family names for their children, trusting they would develop qualities and talents from their namesakes.

Viking families set great store by their ancestors, believing they had a great influence over them, even from the far-off lands of the dead. They had a deep respect for death and took cremation and burial rites very seriously. The dead were equipped with their possessions and sufficient food and drink for their journey to the afterlife. Poor people would be buried with a single ax or knife, whereas wealthy Norsemen and women were often laid to rest with several possessions and all manner of luxuries, including sacrificed servants, dogs, or horses in oval graves marked with piles of stones. Some eminent warriors were buried in their longships, and wealthy Danish women have been discovered buried in wagons. Swedish Vikings were more likely to be cremated, with their ashes contained in a clay vessel rather than buried beneath a marked mound.

Viking society was very much based on hospitality. Norse families enjoyed great feasts and celebrations together, and it was considered a point of honor to never turn a stranger away. Young women could be betrothed at the age of twelve, with a celebration that lasted days, followed by a wedding feast during which a great deal of ale and mead would be enjoyed. From art and carvings made at the time and stories handed down through the generations, it is evident they enjoyed wrestling, sports, and games. They played music and sang as part of their festivities.

Since the Vikings weren't Christians, they had little regard for the consequences of ransacking the holy and sacred places of the "new" religion, viewing them as nothing more than badly defended buildings that, more often than not, contained treasure. As pagans, they often missed out on lucrative trading arrangements that Christian merchants agreed upon with each other and were, like Muslim traders, discriminated against for their beliefs. Due to the Vikings' well-earned reputation for violence, pillaging, and ransacking that would last for centuries, merchants from outside Scandinavia were, unsurprisingly, often unwilling to enter into trading partnerships with them.

Viking raids were so brutal and had become so feared that, in 865, the people of Kent (in the south of England) offered to hand over their riches on the condition the Vikings didn't go ahead with the pillaging. This was a revelation for the raiders. They quickly introduced a levy for their regular targets that became known as the Danegeld, which was essentially a payment or tribute to the Vikings so that they would leave a certain region alone. This continued throughout the 10th and 11th centuries. In 991, during the reign of King Æthelred II the Unready, his subjects were taxed to raise ten thousand pounds (in weight) of silver to be handed over to the Vikings. And it didn't end there; three years later, the Vikings returned and were paid another sixteen thousand pounds. In 1002, they came back for twenty-four thousand pounds of silver.

This was a massive amount to hand over, and it could not continue. The Anglo-Saxons were taxed to the hilt and simply could not afford to pay more. The country was bankrupt, the poor were starving, and the people were beginning to question their king's leadership. Alarmed, Æthelred the Unready gave the extreme order that all Viking settlers who remained in England were to be slain on November 13th, 1002, Saint Brice's Day. Thousands of Scandinavians were killed, including the sister of Sweyn Forkbeard, King of Denmark, who swore revenge when he learned what had happened.

The Vikings returned in 1006, and Æthelred was forced to hand over another thirty-six thousand pounds of silver. In a desperate attempt to finally rid his country of the Viking menace, he hastily built a fleet of ships to defend his shores. However, the English proved to be poor sailors in comparison to the Norsemen, and the Vikings had little difficulty in dealing with them. In 1013, Sweyn and his son Canute (also known as Cnut) arrived to take the English throne. Æthelred fled to France.

However, it would be a short reign. After five weeks, Sweyn died of apoplexy, and Æthelred made his return. Canute returned to Denmark, where his brother, Harald II, had been crowned king. Still, Canute had not given up on the English throne. He returned to England in 1016 after raising a formidable army. On his arrival, he learned that Æthelred had died, so Canute managed to get himself elected as the dead king's heir.

As the self-styled "King of all England and Denmark and the Norwegians and some of the Swedes" (used in a letter to his subjects on the occasion of his coronation), Canute is remembered in medieval texts as a fierce Viking warrior and a wise and capable king. He helped restore prosperity to England, albeit after murdering many of the English lords and possible claimants to the English throne.

The Viking Age is considered to have ended in 1066. Just as it had started with the raids on Britain, it drew to a close when the raids stopped at the time of the Norman invasion. Earlier that same year, the Norwegian king, Harald Hardrada, who had left his shores hoping to fight for the English crown, was killed on English soil at the Battle of Stamford Bridge.

By then, the majority of Scandinavians had abandoned their pagan beliefs, having been converted to Christianity. The church did not look kindly on raiding. In the Icelandic saga *Hitdælakappa*, King Olaf tells Björn of Norway to give it up: "Though you feel it suits you well, God's law is often violated." In any case, all the usual targets had become fortified and were far better defended than they had been in the late 700s.

The Norse gods and heroes were not completely abandoned, though. Even today, a small number of people in Denmark still follow the old religion in a similar war to the Vikings, out in the open air with offerings. Some of the ceremonies have been passed down through the generations, and in recent years, there has been a resurgence of paganism in Iceland. The stories of the deities that fascinated and enthralled the Vikings have developed into the Norse mythology that continues to delight readers today.

Chapter Two: A Viking Legend: Grettir the Outlaw

In the Middle Ages, the people of Iceland developed a tradition of collating detailed family histories in the form of long sagas written in prose form. One of these, *The Saga of Grettir the Outlaw* or *The Saga of Grettir the Strong*, was written in the 13th century and relates the story of a Viking hero.

The saga is divided into three parts. The first thirteen chapters relate the lives of Grettir's great-grandfather, Önundur, a Viking raider who lost a foot while fighting against Norwegian King Harald Fairhair in the Battle of Hafrsfjord (sometime between 872 and 900). The king was victorious, and his enemies, including Önundur Tree-foot (as he was then known), fled from Norway to Britain and Ireland. After fighting against King Kjarval of Dublin, Önundur returned to Norway before setting sail for Iceland, where he settled for good.

The saga then moves to the son of Önundur Tree-foot, Thorgrim Grey-head, and his son, Ásmundar, the father of Grettir.

Ásmundar and his wife Asdis had a farm at Bjarg, where they raised their two sons, Atli, a quiet and serious boy, and Grettir, who was born around 997 CE. Grettir was a difficult character. Even as a child, he was rebellious and truculent but also remarkably strong. He is described as having red hair, freckles, and wide eyes. Though his mother loved him very much, his father was wise to his son's nature and knew he was trouble. Ásmundar and Asdis also had two daughters: Thordis and

Rannveig.

Grettir was not much use on the family farm. When he was fourteen, he was sent in his father's place to the Althing (an annual Icelandic government assembly). One morning, he and the other delegates awoke to find their horses had been let loose and their food stolen. Grettir quickly rounded on one of his companions, Skeggi, and accused him of the crime.

Skeggi responded by drawing his ax. Grettir killed him in the fight. Realizing the seriousness of his actions, he claimed the man must have been killed by a troll, but the other delegates were not convinced. Grettir eventually confessed.

Despite his parents offering weregild (blood money) as compensation for the loss of Skeggi's life, Grettir was banished for three years. Before he left, his mother gave him her grandfather Jökul's short sword, or *sax*, sometimes known as Jökulsnautr ("Jökul's gift") since it was a family heirloom, after Ásmundar refused to give him his.

So, Grettir sets sail for Norway. He does little to help crew the ship until there is a leak. Using his great strength and skill, he manages to repair it. Soon afterward, they hit a rock and the ship sinks just off the Norwegian coast where a local landowner, Thorfinn, helps the ship's crew and passengers to safety. Most of the travelers head south, but Grettir chooses to stay with Thorfinn and his family.

One night, Grettir sees an ominous fire in the distance. When he asks about it, he is told that it is the ghost of Thorfinn's father, Kárr inn gamli, haunting his burial mound. Grettir decides to investigate and tunnels into the barrow. In the burial chamber, which is full of riches, is a *draugr*—an undead, zombie-like creature. It is the undead Kárr inn gamli. The *draugr* quickly attacks Grettir.

As they grapple in the burial chamber, Grettir manages to draw Jökulsnautr, his mother's sword, and slices the *draugr*'s head from its body. He returns to the farm with the treasure from the barrow to tell Thorfinn he has defeated the ghost of his dead father. Grettir asks for a particular sword he has found amongst the grave goods, but he is told he will have to earn it.

Sometime later, Thorfinn is away when a small ship of strangers arrives. They tell Grettir they have come to settle a grievance against Thorfinn. To the horror of Thorfinn's wife, Grettir brings them to the house and gives them copious amounts of alcohol until they are very drunk. Then, he guides them to a large outbuilding and locks them in there. Thorfinn's wife, realizing what he is doing, gives him weapons and armor. Grettir goes back and kills them all. When Thorfinn returns, he hands him the sword he had asked for and swears an oath of lifelong friendship.

Grettir leaves Thorfinn's farm to spend the winter as a guest of a wealthy landowner called Thorkell. He soon makes an enemy of one of his host's men, Björn, who is from a very reputable family but is, as far as Grettir is concerned, very self-important and boastful. The two men take an instant dislike to one another.

Soon after Grettir's arrival, a savage, giant brown bear starts rampaging through the area, audaciously killing livestock in front of the farmers and terrorizing the people. When this monster kills cattle and men on Thorkell's land, his men set out to find its lair.

Its den is on a cliff overlooking the sea. The den is only accessible by a narrow path that is precariously close to the precipice. Grettir's enemy Björn boasts that he will kill this bear, but as he makes his way along the path, he hears the huge beast growling and snoring as it sleeps in his den. Björn lays in wait outside, covered by his shield. As time passes, he falls asleep.

The bear awakens and ambles out of its cave, ready to attack another farmer's flock or herd when it espies Björn. With its massive paw, the bear swipes at the shield to send it tumbling over the cliff. Björn manages to scramble to his feet and flees, narrowly escaping the beast's attention.

He returns to Thorkell, full of bluster, where it is decided a posse of eight, including Grettir, will go to slay the bear. They negotiate the perilous path and try to attack the bear in its den. This proves quite a challenge. Grettir takes off his fur cloak to engage in the fighting, while Björn urges the men to fight it while he remains behind, well out of immediate danger. Björn then flings Grettir's cloak into the melee.

The men give up on their fight, and as they start to leave, Grettir realizes he cannot find his fur. It seems that the bear has hold of it. Björn accuses Grettir of throwing it in there himself in order to go back and kill the bear by himself and claim the glory.

Of course, Grettir goes straight back into the cave and grapples with the ferocious bear. Using Jökulsnautr, he manages to slice one of the bear's paws off. Then, as it comes at him, Grettir seizes it by its ears and pulls its head back so it can't sink its teeth into him. This was, he said afterward, his greatest feat of strength.

Grettir and the bear fall from the path and down the cliff, with the bear tumbling to the beach below, sustaining serious injuries. Grettir lands on top of it. He draws his sword and plunges it into the beast. He then climbs the cliff to collect his battered and torn cloak and the bear's severed paw before returning to Thorkell's.

The men are feasting by the time he returns, and they laugh at Grettir in his ragged fur until he puts the paw on the table. He tells Björn it is time he should start giving him respect, but Björn makes it clear that he will not. However, Thorkell has had enough and tells them to put aside their grievances while they are under his roof.

The next spring, Grettir goes north with Thorkell's men while Björn sails to England. The two men meet again at Trondheim in the autumn while heading back to enjoy Thorkell's hospitality. Grettir is delighted with the opportunity to sort out their differences once and for all. After attempting to avoid a fight and then being accused of cowardice, Björn has little choice but to fight Grettir. Grettir kills him.

Björn's men rush ahead to tell Thorkell, who is saddened but not particularly surprised. Grettir returns to Thorfinn's farm. After explaining what he has done, his friend sagely realizes he will need his support.

Björn's brother Hjarrandi is Jarl Sveinn's bodyguard, and he complains bitterly to him about what Grettir has done. The jarl summons Grettir. Although Grettir admits he had been provoked, the jarl decides he must pay weregild to Hjarrandi.

This outcome is not what Hjarrandi had hoped for. So, while Grettir is out and about, he sets upon him, determined to avenge his brother. But Grettir is too strong for him and kills him and his men. Jarl Sveinn is furious and brings a charge of manslaughter against Grettir, who promptly leaves for Iceland, his banishment almost at an end.

While Grettir is struggling to settle into his new life, he hears about a farmer whose pastures are haunted by a wight (another zombie-like, undead entity). To rid himself of this horrible creature, he had hired a very large and strong Swedish shepherd named Glam, who managed to kill the wight but had been killed in the process. When the farmer and his men found Glam's body lying in the snow, they found it impossible to move him, so they were forced to build a mound around him in the pasture.

Soon afterward, Glam became a horrible revenant (another dreadful, undead creature). He starts haunting the local community, killing their animals and banging on roofs during the night. After he kills the farmer's daughter, Grettir offers to help, despite being warned against it.

The revenant Glam kills Grettir's horse soon after his arrival. On the third night, Glam lifts the roof from the farmhouse and steps inside. Grettir quickly makes his attack. As they wrestle, they destroy everything in the hall until Grettir uses all of his strength to force Glam out through the doorway, wrecking the whole of the exterior wall.

As Glam falls to the ground, realizing his end is near, he glares at Grettir, his eyes glowing in the night. Glam utters a curse, vowing that Grettir will never grow any stronger and that his great and heroic deeds will only gain him hatred and exclusion. These words have a great impact. Unable to forget Glam's glowing eyes, Grettir becomes terrified of the dark.

Trying to put Glam's curse behind him, Grettir learns that the new king, Olaf II Haraldsson, is putting together a troop of elite Icelandic warriors and adventurers–a perfect fit for him. Grettir sets out in midwinter to present himself at the king's court.

On the way, the conditions quickly deteriorated. Grettir, frozen after fording an icy river, beaks into a house in search of fire. Unfortunately, when the people inside see a huge man covered in ice, they think he is a troll and fight him, throwing firebrands at him. In the confusion, the house is set alight, and all those inside are killed, including two sons of a popular local chieftain named Thorir.

Despite it being an accident, Thorir is bent on revenge. He makes sure Grettir has no chance of impressing the king, and matters are not helped when Grettir loses his temper and kills a man whose brother, in revenge, kills gentle Atli back in Bjarg.

The worst is to come. When Grettir returns to the family farm, he finds his father has also died and learns that Thorir has petitioned that year's Althing for him to be declared an outlaw. It is too late for him to offer any kind of defense; the sentence has already been passed.

After killing Atli's murderer and with an even higher price on his head, Grettir is forced to spend many years on the run, often in disguise, relying on old friends and kind strangers since his fear of the dark makes it difficult for him to endure hiding in the wilderness. He spends several years in a glacier-lined valley ruled by a friendly giant and his daughters, but eventually, he becomes restless. He knows Thorir will not give up his quest for revenge and will send assassins to hunt him down.

He hears about a lady called Steinvör who is being plagued by a malevolent troll that has taken her husband and his servant. Introducing himself as Gestur, Grettir offers to help and remains at her estate while she attends Yuletide Mass. When she fears she cannot go because the river is too high, Grettir carries her and her daughter over his left shoulder and crosses the raging torrent, pushing away great lumps of ice with his right arm.

Once they are safely on the other side, Grettir returns to the house and prepares to fight the trolls. As he waits, the doors fly open. A huge troll woman enters, eyes blazing. When she sees Grettir, she attacks. The two of them fight hard all night, leaving a trail of destruction behind them. The troll woman drags Grettir out of the house to a deep gulley by a waterfall, where, exhausted, he wildly swings his sword in a final attempt to stop her from dragging him in. Grettir cuts off her arm. She falls backward into the gulley and disappears.

After returning to the farmhouse, he and another man go to see if they can find Steinvör's husband, who might be in a cave behind the waterfall. His companion holds onto a rope while Grettir abseils down the cliff face.

Grettir dives into the deep gulley behind the waterfall and enters the cave. There, he finds a large fire with a giant stretched out beside it. As soon as the giant sees Grettir, he jumps up and snatches a wooden staff. Grettir manages to defend himself with his sword. When the giant reaches for a better weapon, Grettir slashes at his body and leaves a wound so deep and large that the giant's bowels fall out of his body and into the river.

When Grettir's waiting companion sees the bloody entrails being carried downstream, he believes they must be Grettir's and goes back to the farm to tell Steinvör of his death. Meanwhile, Grettir finishes off the stricken giant and then creeps farther into the cave, where he finds the bones of two men and a great deal of treasure. He puts them in a bag and makes his way to the bottom of the cliff. Since no one is there to help him, he is forced to haul himself up the rock face.

He reveals his true identity to Steinvör and hands her the remains of her husband and his servant and the treasure. She gives him a home until Grettir hears that Thorir's men are closing in on him. He goes back to Bjarg for the last time to tell his mother he is going to Drangey, a fortress on an island at the northern tip of Iceland. It is uninhabited and surrounded by cliffs. Drangey is only accessible by ladder.

Grettir's fifteen-year-old brother Illugi decides to go with him, but their mother knows it will end badly for both of them. They arrive at Drangey with another companion, Glaum, and make themselves at home. However, the families that own the island are far from pleased. They elect Thorbjörn Angle to get them to leave, and he makes several attempts to do this.

By this time, Grettir has been an outlaw for nineteen years. When the Althing decrees that he will soon be free since no man can be an outlaw for more than twenty years, Thorbjörn Angle is ordered to get rid of him before then, or he will lose his share of Drangey.

Thorbjörn consults his foster mother, Thurid, who is a witch, and she agrees to go with him to persuade Grettir to leave. However, when she starts to curse him, Grettir throws a rock at her that breaks her leg. Furious, she is forced to use her dark powers. She finds a tree trunk and carves blood runes into it before setting it out to sea.

On the island, Grettir sees this log a few times. He is suspicious of it, though, and doesn't bring it ashore. Glaum, however, doesn't realize and thinks it will make good firewood. When Grettir tries to cut it for firewood, the ax bounces off it and hacks into his leg.

The wound itself is compounded by the witch's blood runes, and Grettir grows weaker as Thorbjörn and his men storm the island. Glaum, who has already proved a liability, has forgotten to lift the ladder.

Illugi fights like a Trojan, but he can't fight them all. When Thorbjörn reaches Grettir, he finds he has succumbed to his cursed wound. The great, if unfortunate, warrior has died.

Thorbjörn kills Illugi in the hope of preventing a revenge killing and takes Grettir's head to make his claim for the bounty that Thorir had promised. However, when it becomes evident that his death was due to witchcraft, Thorir refuses to pay.

The long saga doesn't end with Grettir's death. His half-brother Thorsteinn Dromund (his father's son with his first wife, Rannveig of Tunsberg in Norway) begins a quest to avenge him, but the action moves from the Viking realms to Constantinople.

Chapter Three: A Guide to Norse Deities

The medieval people of Scandinavia put their faith in a complex system of deities that had various responsibilities over the different aspects of people's lives. Unfortunately for historians and scholars, contemporary Norse-written accounts are practically non-existent. Viking culture passed their history and stories down orally. Decisions, information, and deals were passed along and made by word of mouth. This system worked well since a Norseman's or Norsewoman's word was their bond.

In 98 CE, Roman general Tacitus wrote *Germania*, his study of the culture and customs of northern Europe that gives the earliest account of what has come to be known as Viking (or Norse) mythology. Through Roman trade with Scandinavia, he understood that these people worshiped a pantheon of gods and goddesses, some of whom could be compared to Roman deities.

Tacitus noted that Odin (Woden) was the main god and that animal and human sacrifices were made to him on a particular day of the week, Woden's day, which would become Wednesday. Similarly, Thor (or possibly the god Tyr) was worshiped on Thursday, and Frigg (or Freyja) was worshiped on Friday.

Around this time, the first discovered runestones were being crafted. The Futhark characters were generally used to commemorate and record heroic details about the lives of the great and the good in Norse societies. However, most of the runestones were carved around the time of

Scandinavia's transition to Christianity and thus pay homage to Jesus and the Virgin Mary rather than Odin and Freyja. There are a small number of pagan stones that give a little insight into the old religion.

Modern understanding of Viking mythology chiefly relies on two books: the *Prose Edda* and the *Poetic Edda*. Since Scandinavia was almost exclusively Christian at the time these texts were compiled, the stories had evolved and become intertwined with biblical stories and messages, as well as a scattering of other pagan myths. (In the prologue to the *Prose Edda*, for example, the Norse gods are connected with the surviving heroes at the fall of Troy.)

The title page of a later edition of the Prose Edda.
https://commons.wikimedia.org/wiki/File:Edda.jpg

The *Prose Edda* was written by the Icelandic historian and politician Snorri Sturluson, probably in 1222 or 1223, as a reference to help young poets understand the complex meters of early skaldic poetry and the myths from the Scandinavian oral tradition. It consists of a prologue and three parts. In the *Gylfaginning* ("The Beguiling of Gylfi"), he describes Gylfi, a king of Sweden, visiting Asgard to question the gods. They explain their creation, many of their exploits, and the prophecy of the end of days known as *Ragnarök* ("Twilight of the Gods").

Although the *Prose Edda* is the most valuable resource, at the time of its writing, Snorri was engaged in an attempt to unify Iceland and Norway under the rule of King Haakon IV Haakonsson. Certain passages in the *Prose Edda* could be seen as an attempt to gain hearts and minds with a common cultural identity.

The *Poetic Edda* was written in the second half of the 13th century. It is a collection of mythological poetry composed throughout the Viking Age. None of the poems are attributed to an author, and it is believed that it is an anthology. Several versions still remain, including the treasured *Codex Regius*, which includes thirty-one poems.

These sources provide the stories of many Norse gods and goddesses whom the Vikings trusted for guidance and their well-being. As well as overseeing the lives of men and women, these mystical beings had their own trials and tribulations to deal with. Some of the most common themes include grueling searches for wisdom, the paramount value of honor and heroism, and coping with or executing theft and trickery.

There were three clans, houses, or races of these higher beings. Although they descended from the same ancestors and had inter-clan relationships, they were markedly different in their values and societies. They frequently clashed and even waged wars against each other.

The central, dominant pantheon (at least to humankind) was the Æsir in Asgard. The Æsir were gods and goddesses with the qualities to provide inspiration, comfort, and awe to the Vikings who revered them.

The Æsir

The Æsir are sometimes known as the sky gods. They are the higher pantheon of gods and goddesses in Viking mythology, and they reside in Asgard. They are immortal as long as they continue eating golden apples kept by Idunn, the goddess of spring, youth, and rejuvenation. When she was abducted along with her precious basket of apples by the jötun named Thiazzi, the inhabitants of Asgard aged and grew grey until she was rescued and returned to her orchard. Unlike deities in other polytheistic religions, Norse deities can be killed.

These Æsir gods and goddesses possess the qualities admired and valued by the Vikings, and their flaws and frailties could, for the most part, be identified with, accepted, or understood by the average person. The Æsir are associated with human qualities and concerns like war, strength, and society. There are many more named Æsir gods and goddesses than in the second pantheon, the Vanir, or the Jötun frost giants.

The principal Æsir god in Norse mythology was Odin (also known as Wōden in Old English, Wuotan in Old High German, and Wuodan in Old Dutch). The "All-Father" is the god of war and the dead. He is also the god of wisdom, poetry, and magic. He is the central figure in the Viking faith and rules over Valhalla, where the souls of great warriors are welcomed after they die. In his pursuit of knowledge, Odin frequently gains lovers with whom he fathers children.

Frigg, his ever-patient wife, is the queen of the Æsir and the benevolent goddess of motherhood. She is the mother of Baldr, Hod, and Hermod. In his work, Snorri suggests that Frigg is not averse to the odd extramarital affair. In the *Ynglinga Saga*, when Odin was absent from Asgard, he left his brothers, Vili and Vé, to rule in his stead. During that time, they regularly slept with Frigg.

Thor (Germanic for "thunder"), the son of Odin and the jötun goddess Jörð, is the mighty, hammer-wielding god of lightning and thunder. A fierce warrior, he is resilient and powerful. With the help of Mjölnir, his enchanted hammer, he is even able to fly. In some of the myths, he is susceptible to trickery and has been prosaically described as a "bonehead." However, these stories provide humor and a sense that at least one of the Æsir is not so different from humankind. Thus, he is regarded as a friend to man.

Sif, Thor's wife, is a goddess of the earth and family. She is known for her beauty and, in particular, her wonderful golden hair. Her son Ullr (Thor's stepson) is a particularly handsome god associated with skiing and winter. Sif and Thor's daughter Thrúd ("strength") is the goddess of battle. Modi ("wrath"), their son, is the god of wrath and was closely connected with the fearsome and ferocious Norse warriors known as berserkers. Magni ("mighty"), Thor's son by the jötun Járnsaxa ("Iron Dagger"), is a great warrior.

Thor's half-brother, the divine, Galahad-like Baldr ("prince"), is not as easy to relate to with his innate goodness, light, and unceasing joy. Nanna ("mother"), his wife, is associated with motherhood and is devoted to her wonderful husband. In some Danish myths, she was originally human and the lover of Baldr's blind brother Hodr ("warrior"). Nanna's sister, the gentle Lofn ("comforter"), is the goddess of forbidden love, adultery, and secret marriages, permitted by Odin and Frigg to bless marriages that have been banned. Another sister, the faithful Snotra ("clever"), serves Frigg and is associated with self-discipline and caution. The fourth sister, Sigyn ("friend of victory"), is the long-suffering wife of Loki and mother to Narfi and Váli. She is the goddess of kindness, patience, and devotion.

Other goddesses include Eir ("mercy"), who oversees medicine and childbirth and lives with her healers on Lyfjaberg, a hill where they await human *blót* offerings in exchange for their attention. Gefjun ("generous one") is a goddess of agriculture, particularly the harvest, and Syn ("refusal") is another handmaiden of Frigg. She is associated with rejection, refusal, and enforcing boundaries.

Fulla ("plenitude"), who also waits on Frigg and is responsible for her jewelry and footwear, is the goddess of secrets. The *Prose Edda* recounts that Sjöfn, the goddess of affection and friendship, is another dedicated companion of Frigg. Hlin (Old Norse for "protector") is often depicted with a sword and shield. She provides sanctuary for those Frigg decides to save and is the goddess of compassion, solace, and support. Gná, the goddess of wind transition and change, serves as Frigg's messenger and rides the flying horse Hófvarpnir ("Hoof-thrower") over the seas.

Tyr, another of Odin's sons, is the god of justice and resolution, while the goddess Var is responsible for overseeing promises and agreements with the power to punish those who break their oaths. Forseti, the son of Baldr and Nanna, is the god of peaceful negotiations. He supposedly had a courthouse in which he settled disputes with a flourish of his golden ax. The god Bragi is Asgard's wordsmith and poet. He is the husband of Idunn.

The Vanir

The Vanir gods and goddesses hail from Vanaheimr, a natural world of infinite beauty. It is a world of green woodlands and expanses of clear, calm waters. The Vanir are chiefly associated with fertility and magic. The Vanir women practice *seidhr* (also spelled as *seiðr* or seidr), a spiritual means of healing and prophecy capable of influencing the future. The

Vanir are ethereal, introspective beings. Because there are fewer known Vanir deities than those of the Æsir, it is possible most of their stories have been forever lost.

Although the houses of the Æsir and Vanir exist peacefully alongside one another, this was not always the case. There was a long period of war that started when the Vanir goddess Gullveig visited Asgard. Odin and some of the other gods took an intense dislike to her because she cared for nothing but gold and riches. After a while, they became so sickened by her that they attacked her with spears and then threw her onto the fire. After it seemed she had burned away to nothing, she stepped out of the flames, reborn. So, they tried to burn her again, but the same thing happened. She survived a third fire, and that was enough for the Æsir to believe she had powers of witchcraft.

The Vanir gods and goddesses were, unsurprisingly, appalled at this treatment of one of their own and swore vengeance on the Æsir. Odin, from his all-seeing throne (Hlidskjalf), saw that the Vanir were preparing to fight, so he aimed his spear at them. This was the start of the first war of the world, at least according to the Vikings.

The Vanir used magic and spells to fight against the Æsir, who counterattacked with weapons. After a long time, it became clear that neither side was close to victory, so the leaders met to try and work out the way forward. After arguing about the origins of the war, airing their grievances about the various methods employed, and claiming they were due reparations, the two groups agreed that it would be better for the two houses to integrate so they could live peaceably and unified. Two of the Vanir leaders, Njörd and his son Freyr, came to Asgard. They were accompanied by Njörd's daughter Freyja. The Æsir sent the wisest of their gods, Mímir ("the rememberer" or "the wise one") and Hœnir to Vanaheimr.

To seal the end of the Æsir-Vanir War, each of the gods and goddesses spat into a pot in a solemn gesture to bond the two houses. This created the god of poetry, diplomacy, and inspiration: Kvasir. Although he was just as much an Æsir, he is more associated with the Vanir, perhaps because of his otherworldliness and his propensity to wander and roam while sharing his wisdom.

Initially, the Vanir welcomed their Æsir representatives. They even made Hœnir one of their leaders. However, since he always deferred to the wise Mímir, they grew suspicious and thought perhaps the Æsir had tricked them. When their doubts turned to anger, they seized Mímir and sliced off his head. They sent the head to Odin. The wise god wrapped the head in special herbs and spoke charms to it until it was enchanted enough to speak with him and share his secrets.

Njörd ("force" or "power") was the god of the sea, fishing, and mild weather. According to the *Ynglinga Saga*, he married his own (unnamed) sister, who became the mother of his two children. After his second marriage to the jötun maiden Skadi ("shadow"), the couple left Asgard to live at Skadi's father's hall in the snowy mountains. It only took nine nights for Njörd to realize he could not bear the bleak, endless winters and the howling wolves. So, they returned to his lakeside hall of Noatun. Skadi found it just as difficult to settle there, so after another nine days, they agreed to part. Skadi–a goddess associated with skiing–later became one of Odin's lovers.

Freyja ("lady") is the iconic Viking female deity associated with fertility, beauty, love, and war. She welcomes the ordinary soldiers killed in battle to her hall, Fólkvangr, where they can enjoy the lovely and serene surroundings while the warlords and heroes feast at Valhalla. She is not typically depicted with a weapon, but she possesses *fjaðrhamr*, a marvelous cloak made from falcon feathers that allows the wearer to fly or shapeshift into the form of a falcon.

Since Freyja is the goddess of free love and promiscuousness, she is said to have had relations with every god, including her brother. Her husband, the Vanir god Ódr, is associated with recklessness and madness. He prefers to live a lonely life, wandering from place to place, much to his wife's chagrin. Freyja spends much of her time searching for him in disguise while weeping tears of gold. They share two daughters: Hnoss ("jewel"), a goddess of lust and desire, and Gersemi ("treasure"), associated with adornment, cherished items, and friendship.

Freyja's brother and her twin (at least in some accounts) is Freyr ("lord"), the god of sunny weather, prosperity, and fertility. He is thought to be one of the most popular Viking gods; there are a lot of artifacts that bear his likeness. From Odin's high seat, Hlidskjalf, Freyr sees and falls in love with the jötun Gerd. Determined to win her hand, he presents her with some of Idunn's apples as a gift. Eventually, she marries him, but only after he has given away his enchanted sword that can fight on its own. The *Ynglinga Saga* recounts that their son, Fjölnir, became an ancient king of Sweden.

Freyr rides a golden boar that can be seen in the dark. This animal is named Gullinbursti ("golden bristles"). He also has a magical ship that will always find a favorable wind for its sails and needs no mooring since it can be folded up to fit in his pocket. He also has three loyal servants called Skírnir, Byggvir, and Beyla.

Nerthus is another Vanir goddess associated with fertility and regrowth. It is possible that she is the sister of Njörd (and the mother of Freyr and Freyja), but this is by no means certain. Her story is mysterious and vague, but it is known that early northern European tribes held her in great esteem. They would include a wagon draped in white dedicated to her in a traveling procession.

Gullveig ("gold drunk" in Old Norse), whose torture was the cause of the Æsir-Vanir War, is a Vanir sorceress, seer, and goddess of gold and precious metals.

The Jötnar

Jötunheim is traditionally the home of a great tribe (or tribes) called the jötnar (singular jötun). They have superhuman strength and are sometimes described as frost giants, though in other legends, they are described as being of a similar height to humans. (There were some marriages between the inhabitants of Asgard and those of Jötunheim, so it is generally assumed they were of a similar height/species.) Their realm is described as a wintry, remote wilderness with high mountains and dense, inhospitable forests that echo with the howls of wolves.

In the earlier accounts, the jötnar are often very wise and intelligent but have different values than the Æsir and Vanir. Likely because of the influence of Christianity, they developed into hideous and monstrous creatures that were malevolent but often easy to outwit. Over time, many folklorists believe the concept of the jötnar evolved into mountain-dwelling Scandinavian trolls, which are staples of many modern fairytales.

Some of the early jötnar were very beautiful, such as Gerd, the wife of the Vanir god Freyr. In *Skírnismál* (a poem in the *Poetic Edda*), Gerd is described as remarkably lovely, her beauty illuminating the air and seas. After her marriage, she became one of Asgard's goddesses, representing fertility and earthly love. Hrodr, the friendly giantess, wife of Hymir, the trusted friend of Odin and Thor, and (in some stories) the mother of Tyr, is another attractive jötun. Vor (or Vörr), the handmaiden of Frigg, was originally from Jötunheim. Before the Æsir-Vanir War, she was one of Odin's confidants and provided some helpful advice. After she pledged her allegiance to the Æsir, she became the goddess of truth and prophecy.

Beli ("roarer") is Gerd's brother. In *Gylfaginning*, Freyr is forced to fight him to gain Gerd's hand. However, he has to fight Beli without any weapon since he already gave his sword away. Freyr eventually manages to kill Beli with a stag antler.

Thrym is named the powerful king of Jötunheim. He is the ice giant god of cold and ice. In a humorous story about Thor, the mighty god of thunder, attempting to recover his hammer that Thrym has stolen (or found), Thrym's magnificent hall is described, as is the magnificent feast awaiting his guests.

Ægir, the jötun god of the sea and brewing, is a generous host at the great banquets held in his magnificent palace underneath the sea. These feasts are attended and enjoyed by the gods of the Æsir. His wife, the jötun goddess Rán, also personifies the sea but is far more sinister, cruel, and unwelcoming. She is reputed to lure sailors to their deaths with an enchanted net she uses to drag them beneath the waves. In some of the Icelandic myths, she hosts her own feasts for those drowned at sea as long as they are able to pay their way. It eventually became the custom for Vikings to ensure they carried some gold while they were at sea so they could pay Rán if necessary. Ægir and Rán share a son, Snær, the god of snow, and nine daughters, the waves of the sea. These are generally considered to be the collective mothers of the emerald-toothed god Heimdallr, whose father is Odin. Heimdallr (or Heimdall) was gifted with foresight and tasked with the vital role of guarding the enchanted rainbow bridge called Bifröst.

The jötnar are not so much enemies of the gods of the Æsir as they are allies.; In Asgard, the deities strive to create order and clarity for themselves and humankind. Inevitably, there are clashes and conflicts from time to time, which are not always the fault of the jötnar. However, it is important to remember that there were several relationships and marriages between them, most of which led to children.

Chapter Four: The Norse Cosmos: The Dawn of Time

According to the Vikings' religion, in the beginning–before life itself–there was nothing. This empty, yawning void (according to *Grímnismál* in the *Poetic Edda)* was known as Ginnungagap. To the north of this dark expanse of nothingness, a fountain or well eventually emerged called Hvergelmir. Its waters provided the means for the growth of Yggdrasil, the colossal ash tree.

Ash was a tree well known to the Vikings. It is quick to grow with sufficient water and can mature into a tall tree within a decade. Its timber was used by Norse shipbuilders and woodworkers. Ash wood is flexible, shock resistant, and tends not to split, so this species of tree was the natural choice for Yggdrasil, the world tree.

An illustration of Yggdrasil.
https://commons.wikimedia.org/wiki/File:The_Ash_Yggdrasil_by_Friedrich_Wilhelm_Heine.jpg

Yggdrasil's roots extended deep into the very depths of Ginnungagap, eventually reaching the Well of Urd, where the three Norns (or Nornir) reside. The Norns are described in *Völuspá* (the best-known poem in the *Poetic Edda*) as being Urd (the past), Verdandi (the present), and Skuld(the future). These three Jötnar sisters have the power to influence fate. Urd, the oldest, is a wizened old woman who always looks to the past. Verdandi is young and looks straight ahead with a strong and steady gaze. These two sisters weave destiny together while Skuld, the most frightening and who is completely veiled, periodically rips apart their weaving, throwing the cosmos into chaos and confusion. The three of them also carve runes into Yggdrasil that foretell the future.

In *Grímnismál*, Yggdrasil is imagined differently. It has three great roots:

"'Neath the first lives Hel,

'Neath the second the frost giants,

'Neath the last are the lands of men."[2]

Each of the three roots took water from its own well: Urðarbrunnr tended by the Norns, the creation waters of Hvergelmir, and Mímisbrunnr, the well of wisdom.

At the base of Yggdrasil, several snakes evolve and slither around with the dragon, Níðhöggr (or Nidhogg), who bites and chews at the roots to cause damage to the tree.

The excess waters that flowed from Hvergelmir formed the icy, misty realm of Niflheim and eleven rivers of freezing cold water collectively called Élivágar. At the same time, the southern part of Ginnungagap began to grow increasingly warmer until it became Muspelheim, a fiery furnace of flames, thick black smoke, and lava.

This raging heat began to warm the barren, frozen wasteland of Niflheim until small droplets of thawed water fell. As they fell on Muspelheim, they created sparks that flew into the darkness to create stars.

As the fire and ice began to join together, they created a ball of energy that resulted in the creation of the first being, Ymir ("screamer"), a jötun. An alternative version of this myth is that the sparks wielded by the flaming sword of the fire giant Surtr ("the swarthy one") created the celestial bodies and brought about the conditions for Ymir's creation.

In another version of this story, from *Gylfaginning* in the *Prose Edda*, Ymir is not a product of the merging of the elements but was born of the "yeasty" venom called *eitr*, found in the waters of Élivágar:

"Down from Élivágar did venom drop,

And waxed till a giant it was;

And thence arose our giant's race,

And thus so fierce are we found."[3]

---

[2] *The Poetic Edda*. Translated by Carolyne Larrington. Snorri Sturluson. Oxford University Press, 2014.

[3] *The Prose Edda—Tales from Norse Mythology*. Translated by Jesse Byock. Snorri Sturluson. Penguin Classics, 2005.

At the same time, the immense primordial cow Audhumla (Auðumla, "destroyer of deserts") was created. The *Gylfaginning* explains that this hornless cow, similar to those that northern European farmers had bred since prehistoric times, provided four rivers of milk that fed Ymir while she licked the rime from the surface ice for her own sustenance.

Suitably fed, Ymir rested. From each of his armpits came a male and a female being. His legs created a six-headed monster. These were the ancestors of the jötnar.

Meanwhile, as Audhumla lapped at the ice, her warm tongue made it thaw. On the first day, she uncovered the hair of the first god, which had formed beneath the ice. On the second day, his head was revealed, and on the third day, his body could be seen. His name was Búri ("producer"). He was the first of the Æsir and was (according to the *Gylfaginning*) "fair of feature, great and mighty." Thus, Audhumla had an essential role in the formation of both the Æsir and the jötnar.

Búri had a son (by means unknown or unexplained) called Borr ("borer"). While dreaming, Búri had a vision that the jötnar were evil, so he and his son set about ridding the world of Ymir and his descendants. However, as each night fell, the fighting ended without either side achieving a victory over the other.

Borr married a jötun named Bestla ("wife"), the daughter of the giant Bölthorn ("evil- thorn"). They had three sons: Odin, Vili ("will), and Vé ("wish"). Together, the brothers killed Ymir (their maternal great-grandfather) after finally beating their enemy in battle. So much blood poured from the old giant's wounds that all of the jötnar drowned in it, with the exception of Bergelmir ("mountain-yeller"), who would become the ancestor of the future generations of frost giants.

Odin, Vili, and Vé then took Ymir's remains to the center of Ginnungagap to create the world. In the poem *Grímnismál*, Odin recalls how Ymir's blood became the seas; his bones became hills and mountains; his teeth became rocks, stones, and gravel; his muscle and skin sand and gravel; and his hair the trees.

The brothers took his skull and placed it over the world to form the heavens. Four dwarves named Nordri, Sudri, Austri, and Vestri (the compass directions are taken from these four) took the four corners and held it aloft. They captured some of the sparks flying from the swirling furnace of Muspelheim and threw them into the newly created skies and created the sun, moon, and stars so that their new world was no longer veiled in darkness.

Fearing the jötnar might approach this realm with evil intent, Odin, Vili, and Vé took Ymir's eyebrows and formed them into a boundary to encircle the world and keep it safe.

Once they were satisfied their work was complete, the brothers set about creating the first people to live there. They carved a man and a woman from two tree trunks they found lying on the beach. Odin breathed life into them. Vili gave them blood and the ability to see, hear, speak, and reason, as well as a healthy complexion. Not to be outdone, Vé gave them suitable clothing.

However, in the *Poetic Edda*, Odin, Hœnir, and Lódurr found the already-created humans wandering around with no sense or means of understanding. Odin gave them their mental capacity, Hœnir gave them blood, and Lódurr sorted out their complexions. Since Hœnir and Lódurr are not mentioned again and so little is known of them, the first account (the *Prose Edda*) is the version that is generally preferred.

The brothers named the man Ask (Old Norse for "ash tree") and the woman Embla ("elm" or perhaps "water pot" or "vine"). The humans started a peaceful life on the newly created Midgard. After they had spent some time wandering around and exploring their habitat, they found a dwelling already built and waiting for them. They settled down there and tamed the more biddable animals. They also had several children.

As Midgard became more populated with their perfect descendants, Odin made Ask and Embla rulers of the realm. As the years passed, the jötnar, elves, and other beings came to Midgard disguised as humans and had children with the native people. Later generations were corrupted by the cruelty and evilness associated with those beings.

The story of the creation of the sun and moon and the explanation of their movement is accounted for in the *Gylfaginning*. Gylfi, an ancient king of Sweden who traveled to Asgard on a quest for knowledge, met with Hárr ("high"), Jafnhárr ("just as high"), and Thridi ("third"), mystical beings of the Æsir. It is possible these three deities were Odin and his brothers Vili and Vé, but they could also all have been Odin. King Gylfi learns that the sun races through the sky because a savage wolf, Sköll, is in pursuit, ready to devour it. Similarly, the moon is being hunted by another wolf, Hati.

The Wolves Pursuing Sol and Mani.
https://commons.wikimedia.org/wiki/File:The_Wolves_Pursuing_Sol_and_Mani.jpg

These monsters are the sons of a giantess named Hródvitnir, who lives far to the east of Midgard and has given birth to many wolf-like giants. In other accounts, Sköll ("shadow") and Hati ("hatred") are the sons of Fenrir (the son of Loki and the giantess Angrboda). They were born in the Járnvidr ("iron-wood") forest. Since their mother might also have been their paternal grandmother, this lineage might explain their frenzied bloodlust.

The sun and moon deities, Sól and Máni, respectively, were originally human, according to the *Poetic Edda*. When their father, Mundilfari, arrogantly named them after the revered celestial bodies, the Æsir had them banished to the skies. In a more charitable version, the Æsir appreciated their beauty and gave them the great honor of serving the gods.

These two siblings were given the unenviable task of guiding the sun and moon across the sky each day. Sól pulls the sun in a chariot drawn by two horses named Árvakr ("swift") and Álsvidr ("early riser"). Traveling alongside her in the chariot is a man called Svalinn, who holds a shield aloft to protect the people of Midgard from the strength of the sun's rays.

In the *Gylfaginning*, Máni "guides the path of the moon and controls its waxing and waning." He is followed by two younger children, Hjúki ("the one coming to strength") and Bil ("the waning one"), who had been fetching water from the Byrgir well. These two are almost certainly the origin of Jack and Jill of nursery rhyme fame.

The Norse creation myths share several concepts with other cultures. The central, all-important Yggdrasil is similar to the sacred fig tree Aśvattha in Hindu scriptures, the sacred *Erica* tree in which the body of Osiris is held in Egyptian mythology, and the Bodhi (banyan) tree that brought enlightenment to Buddha. There is also the Tree of Life in the Garden of Eden. Also, sacred cow deities like Audhumla are seen in ancient Egyptian myths (such as the goddess Hathor) and in Hinduism as Kamadhenu, the Divine Mother. The story of the two first male and female progenitors is the basis of most religions and creation myths throughout world history.

Of course, we must remember the written sources we depend on for Norse myths (including the *Poetic Edda* and the *Prose Edda*) were produced well after the spread of Christianity, so some of these stories are likely quite different from the original versions.

Chapter Five: Yggdrasil and the Nine Realms

The massive branches of the world tree Yggdrasil, dubbed the "noblest of trees" by Odin in the *Grímnismál*, reached high and wide. A giant eagle is perched at the tree's very uppermost point. On the eagle's beak and between its eyes sits the hawk, Vedrfölnir ("storm pale"). Together, they keep watch over the nine realms of the Norse cosmos.

The dreadful dragon Nidhogg, coiling around Yggdrasil's roots, sends a squirrel named Ratatoskr ("the traveler") to deliver horrible insults to the eagle, which extends its wings and flaps them in anger, causing the tree to shake. The eagle sends inflammatory messages back to Nidhogg, agitating him so that he writhes in fury. This helps to explain conditions like gale-force winds (from the eagle's wings) and earth tremors (from the movement of the snake). In the poem *Grímnismál* in the *Poetic Edda*, Odin reveals there are more snakes "than any unwise ape can imagine" living beneath the roots of Yggdrasil and that the old tree "suffers agony more than men know" as it endures the snakes' venom and the endless gnawing of its bark by four stags named Daínn, Dvalinn, Duneyrr, and Duraþrór.

The three Norns, as well as weaving the destinies of all beings, tend to the tree and bathe any damage and wounds to it with waters from their sacred well of Urðarbrunnr ("well of fates"). In his quest to gain wisdom, Odin visits the Norns to try to understand their knowledge and learn from their runes, the powerful symbols that make up the sacred ancient

Germanic alphabet that hold the secrets and mysteries of the universe. In Skaldic poetry, these runes hold the key to wielding magic.

The Norns carve the fate of all beings into the roots of Yggdrasil using the sacred rune alphabet. As Odin watches them work, he becomes more and more envious of the power and knowledge they possess. When he begs them to share their wisdom, the Norns tell him that they will only reveal themselves to one who is worthy. So, Odin is forced to take drastic action to gain the mystical knowledge he craves.

After impaling himself with his spear, he hangs himself from the branches of Yggdrasil for nine days, insisting that no one must help him or bring him food. For nine days, he stares at the runes and awaits enlightenment. In the poem *Hávamál*, he recalls:

> "I ween that I hung on the windy tree,
>
> Hung there for nine nights full nine; and offered I was,
>
> To Odin, myself to myself,
>
> On the tree that none may know
>
> What root beneath it runs.
>
> None made me happy with a loaf or horn,
>
> And there below I looked;
>
> I took up the runes, shrieking I took them,
>
> And forthwith back I fell."

His sacrifice is successful. On the ninth day, the runes finally reveal themselves to him. Having understood them, he imparts the knowledge he has gained to others during his incessant wandering.

Upon the great tree Yggdrasil are nine realms, including the fortified human world that is Midgard. The concept of these realms is frequently reinforced in both the *Poetic Edda* and the *Prose Edda*, but they are never comprehensively listed or defined, so it has been left to scholars and mythologists to ascertain exactly what these realms were. Thus, there is some ambiguity. Allowing that there are some worlds that overlap and the mention of other possible worlds, it is widely accepted that the nine realms are Asgard, Vanaheimr, Álfheim, Midgard, Svartálfheim, Jötunheim, Niflheim, Muspelheim, and Helheim.

Asgard is the realm of the Æsir. According to the *Prose Edda*, it is in the center of the world and surrounded by Midgard, the human world, with Jötunheim beyond that, suggesting that the nine realms may have been some system of concentric discs with Yggdrasil as a kind of vertical axis at the center.

According to the *Völuspá*, Asgard suffered a great deal of damage during the war with the Vanir and had to be rebuilt. The *Grímnismál* from the *Poetic Edda* tells the story of a jötun disguised as a master builder (in some accounts, he gives his name as Borgarsmidr). He approaches the Æsir with an offer to rebuild Asgard over three winters in exchange for the sun, the moon, and the goddess Freyja. The gods agree, despite Freyja's absolute refusal to cooperate with any such bargain. However, the Æsir demand that it should be completed within a year, believing this impossible target would get Asgard rebuilt without the possibility of losing the celestial bodies and Freyja. The jötun accepts these terms and gets to work. His mighty stallion, Svadilfari ("unlucky traveler"), moves the great boulders to help him, and he works like a man possessed. It is soon clear that the builder is on schedule to finish within the year.

Horrified, the Æsir realize they will have to do something to slow his progress and call upon Loki, the trickster god and unofficial problem solver, for help. Loki, a shapeshifter, transforms himself into a pretty mare in the hope of distracting Svadilfari. The stallion quickly loses interest in helping his master. No longer able to rely on the horse's brute strength, the building slows down. When the builder realizes that he is doomed to fail, he loses his temper and reveals himself to be a jötun, an enemy of the Æsir. Thor swiftly kills him with his hammer, Mjölnir. In another version of this myth, the builder was employed to build a great fortified wall around Asgard rather than the citadel itself.

Loki seriously distracted Svadilfari and ended up bearing Sleipnir ("slippy one"), the eight-legged horse that could travel through the air and over water. It has also been suggested that the eight legs are reminiscent of the pallbearers that carry the dead, possibly since Loki gifted the horse to Odin, the god of the dead.

Odin and Sleipnir from an 18th-century Icelandic manuscript.
https://commons.wikimedia.org/wiki/File:Odin_riding_Sleipnir.jpg

Iðavöllr ("splendor plain"), mentioned twice in the *Völuspá*, is at the center of Asgard. There, "Shrines and temples they timbered high; Forges they set, and smithies ore, Tongs they wrought, and tools they fashioned." There is Gladsheimr ("bright home"), which, according to *Gylfaginning*, is a meeting place for the Æsir with thirteen high seats where the gods meet to hold council–perhaps a little reminiscent of King Arthur's Round Table in Old English mythology. In the *Gylfaginning*, it is described as "a temple in which there were seats for the twelve of them, apart from the high seat of the All-father. This is the largest and best dwelling on earth; outside and in it is like pure gold." Vingólf, "a very beautiful building," is the hall and meeting place of the goddesses of Asgard. It is also on that plain. Baldr's hall, Breidablik, is the most beautiful of the god's dwellings: *Gylfaginning* states "in that place may nothing unclean be." Baldr and Nanna's son, Forseti, the god of justice, has his own silver and golden hall called Glitnir ("shining one"), which is also used as a courthouse for the Æsir.

Asgard is also home to Odin's great hall, Valhalla, and Freyja's hall, Sessrúmnir, where the souls of human heroes and warriors reside. There are several other halls and dwellings in Asgard. Odin himself has several halls. The Valaskjálf ("shelf of the slain") has a shining silver roof and a tall tower in which Odin has his throne that allows him to see over all nine realms.

Thor's hall, Bilskirnir, is described as the largest in all of the nine realms and has more than 540 rooms. The second largest hall is Landvidi, the hall of the god Vídar. He lives there with his mother Gridr. It is unkempt and overgrown with wild grasses. The god of archery, Ullr, has a home near the forest of Ýdalir ("yew dales"), where he can go to collect the best branches for his bows and arrows.

The queen of the Æsir, Odin's wife Frigg, has a hall named Fensalir ("Fen Halls") in the wetlands of Asgard. Njörd, the Vanir god who made his home in Asgard after the peace agreement, has a hall called Noatun ("place of the ships") at the edge of the sea. There, he watches over sailors and fishermen. Sökkvabekkr ("sunken benches"), the hall of Saga, the hospitable goddess of second sight, is a place "where cool waves flow, And amid their murmur it stands; there daily do Odin and Saga drink, In gladness from cups of gold."[4]

Between Asgard and Midgard is the Bifröst, an enchanted burning rainbow bridge that stretches from Asgard to the human realm Midgard. According to *Grímnismál*, Heimdallr, guardian of the bridge and a god who requires less sleep than a bird, has "his well built house" there.

In the *Prose Edda* (specifically, the *Gylfaginning*), there is more information about the Bifröst. It was built by the gods "with art and skill to a greater extent than other constructions" and consists of three colors. Every day, the gods ride their horses across it, apart from Thor, who wades through the boiling waters of the river Körmt to reach Urðarbrunnr, where they discuss the order of the day.

---

[4] *The Poetic Edda.* Translated by Carolyne Larrington. Snorri Sturluson. Oxford University Press, 2014.

The realm of the Vanir, Vanaheimr, is not described in any great detail in the Eddas. It is thought to be a temperate and lush, rather overgrown, forest world, a place that is more natural than the ordered city of Asgard. In *Lokasenna* of the *Poetic Edda*, Loki states that the Vanir god Njörd came eastward to Asgard, which would indicate that the realm of Vanaheimr is positioned somewhere to the west.

The third realm on the highest level of the cosmos is Álfheim ("home of the elves"), also called Ljósálfheimr or Álfheimr. It is home to the Ljósálfar ("light elves"). These beings are closely associated with the Vanir and are "more beautiful than the sun," according to the *Prose Edda*. The god Freyr rules over Álfheim; it was given to him as a gift when he was a child.

Midgard ("middle enclosure") is the realm of humans. It was created by Odin and his brothers from the body of the giant Ymir. It is the world between the heavenly, ordered realms and those of evil and chaos.

The svartálfar ("swarthy elves"), sometimes known as dökkálfar ("dark elves"), inhabit Svartálfheim ("home of the swarthy elves"), also known as Nidavellir or Myrkheim.[5] It is the realm of dwarves. It is a dark, bleak, and unwelcoming terrain, with clusters of underground caverns beneath twisted, gnarled roots. It is below Midgard and above Helheim on the World Tree.

Jötunheim ("world of giants") is the realm of the jötnar or frost giants. The descriptions paint a picture of immensely tall mountains and vast, dark forests. It is not a particularly hospitable place, at least for the Æsir, Vanir, or humans. It is sometimes referred to as Útgardr ("beyond the fence" or "outer enclosure"), which supports the theory of the realms being concentric circles with Yggdrasil as a central spindle. However, it has also been suggested that Útgardr is some kind of major settlement -a kind of capital city- of this realm.

Niflheim ("world of mist"), the first of the two primordial realms that existed before life began, is an icy, frozen land of mist and darkness where creation began. It is sometimes confused with Helheim, which the goddess Hel rules; in some sagas, they do overlap. It is inhabited by ancient ice giants that are presumably different than the jötnar in Jötunheim. It is generally considered a barren wilderness since most life cannot survive.

---

[5] Most sources use svartálfar and dökkálfar interchangeably, but some sources state they are separate.

According to *Gylfaginning* in the *Prose Edda*, it is the location of the well of Hvergelmir, one of the springs at the roots of Yggdrasil, and the frozen rivers of Élivágar that were an important element in the beginning of life.

Muspelheim ("world destroyer"), the second primordial realm, is the domain of the fire giants or demons. Their chief, Surtr ("the swarthy one"), a terrifying giant, guards the border with a flaming sword. It is a smoky, glowing land of flames and volcanos where no one could survive other than the local inhabitants.

The ship *Naglfar*, mentioned in the *Poetic Edda* and *Prose Edda*, is made of dead peoples' untrimmed fingernails. Once it is complete, it will play a role in the final battle of Ragnarök. The character High sagely suggests that it is wise to keep one's nails short and tidy so that the ship will take longer to be built.

In this vein, according to the *Prose Edda*, Surtr will lead the fire giants in the final great battle during Ragnarök: "At the end of the world he will go and wage war and defeat all the gods and burn the whole world with fire." Just as it was a part of creation, Muspelheim is there for the destruction of life.

Helheim ("Hel's world"), at the very bowels of the cosmos, is ruled over by Loki's daughter Hel and is the final destination of the dead. It is said to lay downward and northward and is divided into several areas. Hel's hall is named Eljudnir (Éljúðnir) ("sprayed with snowstorms"). and is situated in Niflheim. Helheim is a bleak and icy landscape, battered by storms of hail and freezing winds. It has high, impenetrable walls. The dead must cross the golden bridge of Gjallarbrú over the river Gjöll to reach her hall. This bridge is guarded by a maniacal jötun giantess called Modgud ("war frenzy"), who decides who shall enter the gates of Eljudnir and prevents anyone from leaving.

Immediately outside the hall is Garm, a vicious and monstrous hound that guards the gates. There is also Fallandaforad, a great pitfall in which Hel has her bed, kör ("sickbed"), obscured by tattered curtains called Blikjandaböl ("gleaming disaster"). There, she is waited on by her servants, Ganglati and Ganglot (both names mean "lazy walker"), who move so slowly that it is hard to see whether they are actually moving at all. They bring her meals on a plate known as "hunger," and she eats it with the knife she calls "famine."

For the very worst sinners, Náströnd ("corpse beach") was their final destination. The souls of these murderers, adulterers, and oath-breakers were forced to wade through venom to a north-facing castle, its roof a mass of writhing snakes. There, they would suffer eternal torment, namely torture by the vile dragon Nidhogg, who sucks the blood from their bodies.

Chapter Six: Odin the All-Father

In Viking mythology, Odin is the god of wisdom, knowledge, poetry, runes, ecstasy, and magic, but he is primarily a war god and is responsible for those who die in battle. As the chief of the Æsir gods and goddesses, he is an extremely complex and multi-faceted character.

As a great warrior, he is said to have never lost a battle (although the end of the first war between the Æsir and Vanir was hardly a resounding victory). After he and his brother created Midgard, Odin traveled extensively throughout all nine realms, involving himself in many wars and battles. The Norse warriors believed that Odin would decide which side would defeat the other and prayed to him for protection and guidance. They made sacrifices to him before going into battle. The ferocious and fearless berserkers, who fought as though they were in a trance and disregarded the most severe wounds, considered him their patron. In Adam of Bremen's text, *Gesta Hammaburgensis ecclesiae pontificum* (*Deeds of the Bishops of Hamburg*), he refers to Odin as Wotan in his description of the Temple at Uppsala and describes him as the god of war to whom people would leave sacrifices during times of conflict.

Although Odin is indisputably the chief of the Norse gods, the *Ynglinga Saga* describes him as "king of the Æsir." Both Tacitus and Adam of Bremen state Thor was the primary god in the Norse pagan religion, so it may not be until the Eddas that Odin became the central father figure of Asgard. He is mentioned in most of the stories in the Eddas, but that could be a result of the influence of Christianity. Many of Odin's experiences are comparable with figures from the Bible, including himself hanging from the world tree Yggdrasil, his contemplations in the wilderness, and his paternal attitude to the people of Midgard.

A 9th-century depiction of Odin.
https://commons.wikimedia.org/wiki/File:Ardre_Odin_Sleipnir.jpg

As well as being the creator, Odin is the father to several gods. Thor, Baldr, Vídar, and Váli are identified as his children in the Eddas. Heimdallr, Bragi, Tyr, Hodr, and Hermód have questionable parentage, and in some accounts, Odin is their father. He is also the founder of earthly dynasties, such as the Burgundian kings in the *Völsunga Saga*. Skjöldr, the legendary Danish king, and King Sæmingr of Norway were also said to be sons of Odin. In 2020, a haul of treasure was discovered in a field in Jelling, Denmark. It included a gold bracteate (pendant) weighing eight hundred grams that dates to the 5th century CE. It is inscribed in runic letters with the owner's name, "Jaga" or "Jagaz," thought to be a chieftain who might have claimed Odin as an ancestor with the words "Odin's man" alongside the image of a man and a horse.

The mother of Thor Odinson, Odin's oldest son, is generally attributed as the earth goddess Jörd. There is some confusion, however, since Jörd has also been listed as Odin's daughter. The goddess Frigg (Odin's wife) is said to be the daughter of Fjörgynn, another name for Jörd. Some of this confusion may have arisen from the name Jörd also being the Old Norse word for "earth."

Odin is described in *Gylfaginning* in the *Prose Edda* as "beloved of Frigg." As his wife, Frigg is queen of the Æsir, and she is the mother of their ill-fated children, Baldr and Hodr.

In one of the *Poetic Edda* myths, Agnar and Geirrod, the young sons of King Hraudung, are out fishing when their boat is blown ashore. A farmer and his wife (who are revealed to be Odin and Frigg) find them and look after them over the winter. The farmer takes a particular interest in Geirrod, while his wife cares for his older brother. The following spring, the old man gives them a boat, whispers something to his favorite foster son, and sends them on their way.

As they reach their home, Geirrod jumps out of the boat and pushes it back to sea with Agnar still aboard, cursing him. "Go wherever the trolls take you," he tells his brother. The enchanted boat sails swiftly away. As Geirrod enters his father's hall, he finds his father had died while he had been away. Since the older brother is lost at sea, Geirrod is crowned king.

One day, Odin is laughing at Agnar's fate while living in a cave with a troll woman and their children. Frigg points out that while Geirrod may be king, he is a bad ruler. He is mean and stingy. Geirrod will not feed his guests if there are too many of them, which is unforgivable behavior to the hospitable, feast-loving Vikings. Odin, unwilling to believe his foster son could be capable of such a heinous crime, makes a wager with Frigg that this simply isn't so. Odin prepares to go and see Geirrod for himself disguised as Grimnir ("shadowed face").

Frigg quickly sends her handmaiden Fulla to tell Geirrod that a malevolent sorcerer is on his way to his kingdom to cause harm but that he will be easy to recognize since no dog will bark at him. When Grimnir arrives, Geirrod sets his dogs on him (as he has done with all of his guests). When the dogs will not so much as sniff at the stranger, Geirrod orders his men to tie up Grimnir and suspend him between two large fires for eight nights in an attempt to make him reveal his intentions. Of course, the disguised god will not speak.

Geirrod's young son, also named Agnar (just like the brother the king had betrayed), takes pity on the prisoner and gives him a drink of mead. By that point, the fire has become so fierce that Odin's disguise has burned away. Odin begins to speak to the boy. He tells him about Asgard and the many names and disguises he has taken.

Agnar reveals the tortured prisoner's true identity to his father. Geirrod, horrified, leaps to his feet to go and free Odin from the fire, but in his haste, he falls upon his sword and is killed. Agnar (the son, not the brother) then becomes king and rules wisely for many years.

Odin is sometimes referred to as the "raven god." His association with these birds certainly predates the Eddas. Artifacts from the Viking Age often depict him with representations of ravens, and in folklore, it is said that their appearance after a sacrifice was a sign that Odin had accepted it. In the *Poetic Edda*'s *Grímnismál*, Odin speaks of his own ravens, Hugin (possibly from the Old Norse *hugr*, meaning "thought") and Munin (from *munr*, meaning "memory"). These ravens fly all over the world each day. When they return, they whisper to Odin, telling him all they have seen.

As well as his bird companions, Odin has two grey wolves, Freki ("the ravenous one") and Geri ("the greedy one"). It has been said that Odin created them for company when he felt lonely during his travels, and they became his loyal guardians. Vikings were encouraged to respect and learn from these animals. Ravens were known for their intelligence, and wolves were as courageous and wise. Wolves had a strong sense of family since they demonstrably took care of all members of their packs.

A great deal of Odin's time is spent in the pursuit of knowledge. In the *Poetic Edda*'s *Völuspá*, the wisest of all of the gods was initially Mímir, a mysterious water deity who lives at the Mimisbrunnr well that provides water for the Jötunheim root of Yggdrasil. (In other stories, wise Mímir was the unfortunate Vanir god whose decapitated head Odin carried with him.) According to the *Völuspá*, Mímir guards this well as it is where "wisdom and understanding were stored." Anyone who drank its waters would be forever enlightened. Mímir drinks from it every morning. When Odin visits, craving knowledge, he has to forfeit one of his eyes for a share.

Mímir pours the water into the Gjallarhorn, one of the Æsirs' most treasured possessions. As well as being a drinking horn, Gjallarhorn is also a musical instrument. In other stories, Gjallarhorn is given to Heimdallr, the god responsible for keeping watch over the realm of Asgard. Once Odin has drunk from the well, he becomes the wisest of all of the gods. Despite losing his eye, he is able to see more than any of them due to his immense knowledge.

In another one of Odin's myths, Kvasir, the eloquent god of poetry and wisdom (who had been formed from the spit of the Æsir and Vanir after the war), had taken to wandering and sharing his beautiful words and cleverness with all he met. When he comes across two particularly horrible dwarfs named Fjalar ("deceiver") and Galar ("shouter"), they kill

Kvasir and drain all the blood from his body, then mix it with honey to make an enchanted mead they call Óðrœrir, the mead of poetry. They store the mead in three containers. When the gods search for Kvasir, the dwarves laugh together and say that he has choked on his own cleverness.

But worried the powerful gods will come after them, the dwarves persuade a giant, Gilling, to take them out to sea. Once they reach deep water, they overpower him, and he falls overboard. Unable to swim, he drowns. When the wicked dwarves return to the shore and tell her that Gilling has been killed in an accident, she cries out in grief. The dwarves dislike the sound of her wailing and kill her by dropping a millstone on her head.

These giants have a son named Suttungr ("heavy with drink"), who seizes the murderous pair when he learns what they have done to his parents. Pleading for their lives, they offer him their three containers of the mead of poetry they made from Kvasir's blood. Suttungr agrees. He hides it under the Hnitbjorg, a mountain, with his daughter Gunnlöd keeping guard.

Odin is determined to drink this mead and gain its powers, so he disguises himself as a farm laborer and goes to Suttungr's brother's farm, where nine men are working hard. Odin offers to sharpen their blunt scythes with a special whetstone. After he has attended to them, the scythes are razor sharp and quickly cut through the hay. The farmhands ask if they can buy the stone, and Odin agrees but cryptically warns them they will have to pay a high price. He throws it into the air. The men scramble for it, and in the tussle, they kill each other with their newly sharpened blades.

Odin then goes to the farm and tells Suttungr's brother that his men have killed each other in an argument. He says his name is Bölverkr ("worker of misfortune") and offers to do all of their work in exchange for a sip of Óðrœrir. The farmer replies that it is not his, but he agrees to speak to his brother.

After working on the farm as agreed, Odin and the farmer go to Suttungr, but the giant will not allow them anywhere near his mead. Odin has no intention of giving up. After making his companion drill through the rock of the mountain, he shapeshifts into a snake and slithers into the hole. He wriggles his way into the chamber where the lonely Gunnlöd is guarding the precious mead.

She initially refuses to give Odin any of it, but after he says he will sleep with her for three nights, she agrees to allow him a small drink from each of the containers. However, after the third night, the containers are empty since each of Odin's sips leaves them completely empty. Ever the charmer, Odin leaves, flying away in the form of an eagle.

Suttungr, realizing he has been robbed, comes lumbering after him. But as they approach Asgard, he is forced to give up his chase. The gods, having seen Odin as an eagle make his approach, set out containers. Odin regurgitates the mead he has swallowed into them. As he does this, some drips from his beak fall onto Midgard, and those who are touched by them become the poets and scholars of the human world.

As well as having an obsession with wisdom, Odin is just as fascinated by enchantments, spells, and less worldly knowledge. In the 10th-century Anglo-Saxon manuscript *Lacnunga*, Odin (as Woden) is mentioned twice in the Nine Herbs Charm, an ancient recipe for a magical spell used for healing and protection. In addition to his ability to shapeshift, he learns the Vanir witchcraft *seidhr* from Freyja and frequently consults völvas and soothsayers for advice.

In the final part of the *Völuspá* (itself translated as the "Witch's Prophecy" or "Sibyl's Prophecy ") from the *Poetic Edda*, an aged seeress reluctantly gives Odin the prophecy for Ragnarök, the end of the world, and the fate of all the deities in the Norse cosmos. Many of Odin's actions are often futile attempts to delay what he believes to be inevitable. His accumulation of the *einherjar* ("army of one," the souls of those killed in battle) at Valhalla, his diligent watchfulness over the nine realms, and his uncharacteristic benevolence and endless patience toward Loki (although they are bound as blood brothers) can all be seen as efforts to avoid the inescapable ending known as Ragnarök.

Chapter Seven: Valhalla and the Afterlife

As well as being the god of wisdom, healing, and poetry, Odin was, more importantly, the god of war and the dead or at least the god of slain great warriors. He welcomed the souls of Vikings who had been killed in battle—the most glorious dead—at his magnificent hall, Valhalla ("Hall of the Slain").

The souls of these most worthy warlords and celebrated soldiers were known as the *einherjar* ("army of one"), and they were destined to fight alongside the Æsir at the final battle of Ragnarök.

Several poems in the *Poetic Edda* (including *Völuspá* and *Grímnismál*) and the *Prose Edda* recount how the *einherjar* are selected from the dead on the battlefield by the Valkyries, an army of female warriors who are armed and wear helmets. They ride (or rather fly) on their horses over land and sea. In some stories, they are known as Swan Maidens because they disguise themselves as swans so they can fly away quickly.

In *Völundarkvida* in the *Poetic Edda*, three brothers who live at Úlfdalir ("wolf dales") notice three women spinning linen at the shore of a lake. When they see their swan garments nearby, the men realize the ladies must be Valkyries. They take them back to their homes, and the three couples live happily for seven years until the Valkyries fly off to battle, never to return.

In some myths, the Valkyries are said to be the daughters of Odin, but in the Eddas, they are more often princesses, the daughters of kings. In the poem *Helgakvida Hjörvardssonar*, a young prince sees nine Valkyries riding past him. One he describes as the "bright faced lady." She is Sváva, the daughter of King Eylimi, and she protects the young prince in many battles.

In the *Völuspá*, a seeress describes six Valkyries: Skuld ("fate"), who carries a shield; Skögul ("shaker"), Gunnr ("war"), Hilda ("battle"), Göndul ("wand-wielder"), and Geirskögul ("spear-bearer"). In *Grímnismál*, eleven more Valkyries are identified by name. It is explained that Skuld is also one of the Norns and has a special role as a Valkyrie since she "always rides to choose the slain and decide the outcome of battle."[6]

The Norse hero Helgi Hundingsbane's story is retold in two chapters of the *Poetic Edda*. Helgi was the son of Sigmundr and Borghildr of Brálund, whose story is included in the *Prose Edda*. On the night Helgi was born, the Norns determined his fate and decided he would be a great prince.

At the age of fifteen, Helgi disguises himself and infiltrates the court of the Saxon king Hunding, the enemy of his people, with an audacious plan to capture and kill him. Before long, the king grows suspicious of Helgi, and he is forced to make his escape in the dress of a bond-woman (a female servant) and hides away in a mill.

Soon afterward, Helgi takes an opportunity to kill King Hunding, which earns him his name, Helgi Hundingsbane. The king's sons demand that he pay them weregild, the blood fine levy due for murder, in lieu of revenge, but Helgi refuses. Instead, he leads his men into battle against these Saxon princes.

After the battle, in which he kills all of the dead king's sons, Helgi rests beneath Arastein ("Eagle Cliff") as Valkyries appear on the battlefield with "bolts of lightning; wearing helmets at Himingvani. Their byrnies [armor] were drenched with blood; and rays shone from their spears."[7] One of them, Sigrún, speaks with Helgi while still mounted on her horse. She tells him how her father has betrothed her to a particularly despicable and ignoble prince, one of the sons of Granmar, king of the Hniflungs, whom

---

[6] *The Poetic Edda*. Translated by Carolyne Larrington. Snorri Sturluson. Oxford University Press, 2014.

[7] *The Poetic Edda*. Translated by Carolyne Larrington. Snorri Sturluson. Oxford University Press, 2014.

she considers to be unworthy of her.

Helgi chivalrously gathers his men together, and they set sail for Frekastein to wage war on Granmar and his armies to save Sigrún from her forthcoming marriage. During the voyage, there is a great storm. Sigrún's intervention with Rán, the volatile sea goddess, saves all of their lives.

Upon their arrival at Frekastein, Helgi's men make their attack on Granmar's forces. As they fight, the Valkyries arrive to help them achieve victory. After it is over, the Valkyries fly away, leaving Helgi and Sigrún to marry.

They have several sons, but they do not live happily ever after. One of Granmar's sons, Dagr, survived, and he is bound by Viking honor to seek revenge on the man responsible for the slaughter of his father and his brothers. He prays to Odin, and after making the appropriate sacrifices and rituals, Odin gives Dagr his spear, which he uses to kill Helgi.

Dagr tries to give his condolences to Sigrún, but she is bereft and curses him, telling him he should spend the rest of his life in the forest eating only rotten meat for his cruelty. Then, she has a barrow prepared for her beloved. However, his soul is already in Valhalla, where he seems quite happy, especially since he has sufficient influence to have his old enemy, Hunding, made to feed the pigs and wash the *einherjars'* feet.

Meanwhile, Sigrún continues to pine for her husband. When a servant tells her she has seen him and his men riding into his funerary barrow, she runs to see for herself. There, she finds Helgi, but he is disheveled, his hair covered with frost, his hands wet, and his body spattered with blood. He tells her this is because her tears of grief continue to fall onto him. They spend the night together in his barrow, but the following day, Helgi returns to Valhalla, leaving Sigrún to mourn alone once more.

In Snorri Sturluson's *Heimskringla*, the best known of the old Norse king sagas, the earthly rituals necessary to prepare a warrior for Valhalla are described. The body was to be laid on a funeral pyre with all his possessions. Sometimes, even his wife and servants would be placed on the pyre so they would be there for him in Valhalla. Afterward, the ashes were to be spread on the ground or scattered on the sea.

Valhalla is described as magnificent and palatial. When the men are called to fight at Ragnarök, some 800 warriors will march out of its 540 doors. The *Poetic Edda* describes Valhalla as "rising peacefully" for the weary *einherjar* who approach its doors. In front of the main entrance stands a tree with red gold leaves called Glasir ("gleaming"), and the gates are guarded by wolves while eagles soar overhead. The hall has "spear-shafts for rafters, it's roofed with shields, mail-coats are strewn on the benches," and there are piles of the possessions that have been buried or cremated with the warriors for their long journey to the afterlife.

According to *Grímnismál*, Valhalla is located in Gladsheimr, and Thor's hall, Bilskirnir, is contained within its walls. In the *Poetic Edda*, an argument between Odin (in disguise as a ferryman) and Thor includes the revelation that the souls of dead thralls (the enslaved or serfs) reside in Thor's fields, Thrúdvangar.

Beyond Valhalla is the decidedly heavenly Gimlé, a world inhabited by angelic light elves. It is in Vidbláinn, a heavenly plain above Asgard. The brave souls that survive Ragnarök will be welcomed there.

Once the *einherjar* arrive at Valhalla, they can enjoy the Vikings' ideal life. There will be permanent and perpetual fighting and epic war games, often to the death. Before the great feast at the end of each day, all wounds are healed, and those who had been slain that day are reborn or at least breathe again.

It is not only the dead *einherjar* that are restored to life. Odin's unfortunate boar Særimner is slaughtered daily to feed this massive army, only to reappear and go through the same process the following day. He is butchered by Andhrímnir, the cook of the gods, then stewed to perfection in Eldhrímnir ("fire-sooty"), a great cauldron.

The feasting warriors also partake in copious quantities of mead that is provided by Odin's goat, Heidrún. She eats the leaves of the Læraðr tree at Valhalla and is milked for this magical mead by the busy Andhrímnir. The Valkyries then serve it. According to the *Prose Edda*, "there are still others whose duty it is to serve in Valhalla. They bring drink and see it to the table and the ale cups ... these women are called Valkyries."[8]

In the *Prose Edda*'s *Skáldskaparmál*, Snorri presents a picture of a dining hall full of atmosphere. There is no lighting other than the gleaming swords of the *einherjar*. During the feasting, Odin does not eat any of the meat. He gives his share to his two wolves, Geri and Freki, his constant companions. He does, however, partake in Heidrún's excellent mead.

---

[8] *The Prose Edda—Tales from Norse Mythology*. Translated by Jesse Byock. Snorri Sturluson. Penguin Classics, 2005.

Although Valhalla is home to some of the fiercest and most brutal warriors, it would seem there are certain expectations in terms of etiquette. In *Skáldskaparmál*, the jötun Hrungnir ("brawler"), on his golden-maned horse Gullfaxi, is beaten in a race against Odin on his eight-legged horse, Sleipnir. When the race ends at Valhalla, Hrungnir is invited inside in the typical Viking spirit of extending hospitality. He quickly becomes inebriated and abusive, offending the assembled Æsir. When he brags that he will take Valhalla back to Jötunheim, they are heartily sick of his boorish company and summon Thor to deal with him. Drunk as he is, Hrungnir craftily reminds him that he is a guest of the Æsir and cannot be harmed. However, he is persuaded to leave Valhalla to indulge in a flyting (battle of words). In some versions of the story, Thor slays him with his hammer, Mjölnir, and takes possession of Hrungnir's wonderful horse.

The Wild Hunt, or Odensjakt ("Odin's ride"), in which Odin, on his horse Sleipnir, leads a great host of Valkyries, ghostly dead warriors, elves, wolves, and hawks in a thundering chase through the deep, dark forests, has been retold in northern European mythology, although there are some variations from region to region. Most Celtic and Germanic folklore describe the hunt as an omen of doom for those who are unfortunate enough to see it, but in Norse mythology, it is never seen, only heard. The ghostly sounds of a jostling crowd galloping at full pelt, hooves thundering, the clashing of armor and weapons, and Odin's hounds baying into the night would certainly be a haunting thing to hear.

Before the advent of Christianity, it was presumed these hunters were in pursuit of a boar or some mystical being that needed rescuing or destroying. Afterward, the hunters had a different quarry and were said to be running sinners to ground or hunting for children who had not been baptized.

The remaining warriors who are not selected by the Valkyries for Valhalla go to Freyja's afterlife, Fólkvangr ("Field of the People"), a peaceful meadow where weary souls can take their rest. It is attested in both the *Prose Edda* and the *Poetic Edda* that Fólkvangr lies within Freyja's hall, Sessrúmnir.

In *Grímnismál*, Agnar learns from the disguised Odin that "Freyja decrees who shall have seats in the hall; The half dead each day does she choose, And half does Odin have." [9] Similarly, in the *Prose Edda*,

---

[9] *The Poetic Edda.* Translated by Carolyne Larrington. Snorri Sturluson. Oxford University Press,

"whenever she rides to battle she gets half her slain."[10]

The difference between the souls selected by the Valkyries for Valhalla and those taken to Freyja's Fólkvangr is not clear, but since the prophecy of Ragnarök calls for the *einherjar* to fight shoulder to shoulder with the gods, their existence at Valhalla can be regarded as a divine training program to prepare them for that time. Those enjoying Freyja's hospitality are, perhaps, the souls of the good and the honorable who lack the ferocity required for that last great battle.

In the old Icelandic *Egill's Saga*, which dates back to 1240 CE and tells the family story of the Viking Egill Skallagrímsson, a woman named Thorgerd says, "I have had no evening meal, nor will I do so until I join Freyja ... I do not want to live after my father and brother are dead." This would suggest that starving oneself to death was considered a sufficiently noble demise for the lower tier of dead heroes in the afterlife.

Freyja has another possible connection with the afterlife for the Norse people. The souls of unmarried women who die become attendants of Gefjon, according to the *Heimskringla* (one of the Old Norse kings' sagas, written by Snorri Sturluson). Although Gefjon is a goddess associated with agriculture in Danish myths, Gefjon was another name for Freyja by Norwegian Vikings. So, it is possible that, allowing for their names being muddled in the mists of time, it is Freyja who takes them. If that was the case, her halls host a rather more mixed crowd than Valhalla.

For those who died at sea (surely an occupational hazard for the Viking raiders), there is no passage to Valhalla. The Norse sea god Ægir is widely accepted to be a jötun, albeit a particularly reasonable and friendly one. His wife, Rán, is sometimes described as his sister or a Vanir goddess, but the two have very different characters and purposes.

Ægir is associated with all the benefits of the sea, such as calm waters and fishing. He is also celebrated for his wisdom. Rán is the dangerous and cruel perpetrator of stormy seas and shipwrecks. She has a great net that she casts out into the depths to ensnare hapless sailors and then drags them down to her realm, where they will remain in her hall.

The Norse legends also suggest a possibility of reincarnation, especially through ancestry. In the *Saga of Hrómundar Gripsson*, Helgi

---

2014.

[10] *The Prose Edda—Tales from Norse Mythology.* Translated by Jesse Byock. Snorri Sturluson. Penguin Classics, 2005.

Hundingsbane and his Valkyrie wife Sigrún were Helgi Hjörvardsson and his beloved Sváva in a previous life and Helgi Haddingjaskati and Kára in the next. There is also the suggestion that some of the dead did not leave their barrows or burial mounds but remained there, body and soul, to watch over their descendants and their homes. In the Icelandic *Eyrbyggja Saga*, there is a story about a shepherd who shares his vision of the mountain Helgafell opening up to receive a dead man (and worshiper of Thor). There, he finds his deceased family feasting and is happily reunited with his dead father.

Finally, there was Hel's realm. This was not quite the hell of Christianity. The *Prose Edda* suggests that all of the dead—other than those selected for Valhalla, Fólkvangr, or Rán's hall—enter Helheim. There are pleasant areas where flowers grow, and there is feasting. Baldr and Nanna are depicted in the seats of honor at one such occasion in *Gylfaginning*. Wicked people do not remain with Hel; they die again to plummet farther into the dreadful realms at the bowels of the Norse cosmos.

Chapter Eight: Freyja, the Goddess for All Seasons

Freyja ("lady") is often considered the archetypal Norse goddess. She is beautiful, ethereal, and strong. She and her brother (sometimes her twin) Freyr were born to Nerthus, the goddess of prosperity and peace. (It was believed that when she was among humans, no conflict or battle would occur.) Their father was Njörd, a major god of the Vanir who helped to oversee sailing, fishing, and prosperity.

Freyja was the goddess of love, fertility, magic, war, and death. She is sometimes referenced as a Valkyrie and even as their leader, being responsible for half of those who died in battle. These men were possibly deemed less heroic than those who headed to Valhalla because they do not appear to play a role in the final battle of Ragnarök and live a peaceful existence under Freyja's care.

There is scant information about Freyja prior to her move from Vanaheimr to Asgard. Since there are so many conflicting stories about her, it is likely that she has become confused with other goddesses, particularly Odin's wife, Frigg, whose name is not too dissimilar to Freyja. Even Freyja's husband's name, Ódr, can easily be muddled with Odin. It has been noted that the entity "Frija" could be a combination of Freyja and Frigg or even the two intertwining into one being. Gullveig, who was possibly the cause or a casualty of the Æsir-Vanir War, and Gefjon, the fertility goddess associated with plowing, have also been interwoven with Freyja throughout the years. The Christian monks who put the myths to parchment were likely not as concerned (or interested) in the goddesses. Since Freyja's name is synonymous with the word "lady," confusion was unfortunately inevitable.

The *Ynglinga Saga*, one of Snorri Sturluson's kings' sagas, presents Freyja as one of the Vanir's leaders in the Æsir-Vanir War. She worked closely with Odin to help oversee the peace settlement and took responsibility for the offering of sacrifices. In the same saga, Freyja is revealed as a völva, a seeress gifted in the mystical practice of *scidhr*, which she introduces to Asgard. (In the *Lokasenna*, she reveals that Frigg is also a gifted shaman who knows the fate of everything.) Freyja has also been seen as a destiny-weaving Norn, probably due to her gifts as a seeress, which is somehow fitting since her true–or original–story has been unraveled somewhere within the many strands of mythology, legend, and folklore.

Just as Odin has his spear and Thor his hammer, Freyja has a marvelous cloak made from falcon feathers that gives the wearer the ability to fly or shapeshift into a hawk. She travels in a chariot drawn by two black or grey Norwegian Forest cats or lynxes and is usually accompanied by her battle swine, Hildisvíni. In *Hyndluljód* of the *Poetic Edda*, one of Freyja's loyal followers (sometimes presented as her lover), Óttar, builds a shrine to her and prays for her to help him discover his ancestry after he has made a wager of everything he owns on the quality of his forefathers. Freyja appears to him and disguises him as Hildisvíni. The goddess rides on Óttar's back as they travel to see the jötun sorceress Hyndla. Freyja forces her to tell Óttar what he wants to know and also to give him a potion, *minnisöl* ("memory cup"), that will ensure all he has been told will not be forgotten. Since he is descended from several great heroes, he wins the bet and becomes a formidable Swedish king.

Despite being arguably the most popular of the Norse goddesses, Freyja exhibits some serious flaws. In *Lokasenna*, when Loki has his meltdown and accuses the Æsir of their many indiscretions and decidedly ungodly behavior, he airs some dirty laundry about Freyja. He states that she has slept with every god and elf present in the hall, which she denies. Freyja insists that he is simply trying to draw attention from his own misdeeds and bad behavior, then tells him to go home to lick his wounds. But Loki is by no means finished. "Be silent, Freyja! Thou foulest witch," he counters and crudely describes an occasion when the gods surprised her and her brother Freyr while they were enjoying sexual relations.

Freyja treasures her magnificent golden and amber necklace, the Brísingamen ("gleaming torc"). In the early 14th century story *Sörla páttr*, written by two Christian scholars keen to discredit the pagan gods and hoping to put an end to the customs being practiced in their names, Freyja is a mortal and one of Odin's favorite and avaricious mistresses. When she hears of a fabulous necklace (clearly Brísingamen, though this isn't stated) that has been created by skilled dwarf craftsmen, she cannot help but go and have a look for herself. When she sees it, she has to have it, whatever the price. The four dwarves agree to give it to her in exchange for her sleeping with each of them.

When Freyja refuses to tell Odin how she came by her fabulous jewel, Loki finds out and tells him. They decide to steal the necklace from her. Loki, a shapeshifter, turns himself into a flea and hops into Freyja's bed. When he finds her sleeping on her necklace, he bites her cheek, and she turns over. Loki then takes the necklace to Odin.

When Freyja realizes she has been robbed, she appeals to Odin. He tells her that he knows exactly how she had procured it and that he will only return it after she agrees to force two great kings to fight against each other in a perpetual war. Whenever one is killed, they will rise again to continue the battle. These bitter hostilities will continue until a Christian savior (namely Olaf Tryggvason, king of Norway from 995 to 1000 CE) will end this state of affairs.

There is certainly a missing myth about the theft of Brísingamen. In the *Prose Edda*, there is a story about how Heimdallr and Loki fight over the necklace while transformed into seals. Thereafter, Loki is referred to as the thief of Brísingamen. There are scenes of a battle between the two (though not as seals) carved onto the walls of an old mead hall and described in the poem *Húsdrápa*, written by the 10th-century historical poet Úlfr Uggason. Brísingamen also appears in the old English epic poem *Beowulf*.

This view of Freyja is countered by her devotion to her husband Óðr ("frenzy" or "inspiration"). The couple had a difficult relationship. Óðr, sometimes attributed as the god of sunshine and summer, is a curious character. He is restless and unsettled. He leaves Freyja for long periods, wandering and exploring foreign lands (like Odin) and enjoying the company of other women.

When he leaves the first time, Freyja is bereft. The land becomes cold and barren, plants and flowers wither, and nothing will grow. As she weeps, her tears fall on the earth and turn into gold. When she can no longer bear to be without him, she sets out to find him. Disguised, she travels from place to place, leaving gifts and blessings to everyone she meets along her way. She dares not reveal herself in case Ódr learns that she is near and flees until, eventually, she finds him one night sleeping underneath a tree. She quietly lays beside him. When he awakes, he is delighted to see her. He has grown tired of his travels but has been worried he would not be made welcome after his absence due to his womanizing. With the couple reunited, the bitter winter melts away, and the world grows more temperate. Flowers begin to bloom, and crops grow again.

In time, Ódr once more grows restless and feels compelled to leave. Again, the world is enveloped by winter snow. But Freyja knows he will be loyal to her and that he will come home. When he does, the warm summer sunshine will return as well.

Freyja and Ódr share two daughters, the beautiful Hnoss ("jewel") and Gersemi ("treasure"), who are possibly one and the same. In *Skáldskaparmál*, Hnoss is referred to as Freyja's "gold-wrapped glorious child" and Freyr's niece. In *Gylfaginning*, there appears to be only one daughter: "Hnoss is the name of their daughter. She is so beautiful that from her name whatever is beautiful and precious is called Hnossir."[11]

Freyja (and Frigg) have probably suffered more than most of the Norse deities during Christianization. Freyja's name, especially in the plants and places named after her, were often replaced with that of the Virgin Mary, perhaps inevitably since Freyja translates as "lady". The wildflower milkwort *Polygala vulgaris*, that was known as Freyja's hair in Scandinavia was later renamed after the Virgin Mary.

Though the confused and vague picture that remains gives Freyja an unworldly and ethereal quality that befits the held view of the Vanir, the Vikings saw her in a much different light. She was revered as a goddess of war and earthly love, and they believed rituals and sacrifices to her were a necessary part of life.

---

[11] *The Prose Edda—Tales from Norse Mythology*. Translated by Jesse Byock. Snorri Sturluson. Penguin Classics, 2005.

Chapter Nine: Thor, God of Thunder

Thor ("thunder"), the muscular and mighty bearded warrior, is synonymous with Viking culture. He holds a special place in the Norse myths as the fearless, hot-tempered, and headstrong warrior and served as an inspiration to the men of Scandinavia in the Viking Age.

As a god, he was known for his benevolence toward humankind. Despite his father Odin being the All-Father, Thor seemed to have been worshiped more than any other Norse god, particularly in Iceland. Representations of his hammer, Mjölnir, have been found carved onto a great number of runestones and Viking artifacts. Thor's role is "defender of Asgard and Midgard," according to *Skáldskaparmal* in the *Prose Edda*. In the myths, he regards the jötnar as his enemy despite his paternal grandmother being the jötun Bestla and having a relationship with another jötun, Járnsaxa, mother of his son Magni. Magni is the only god other than Thor able to lift Mjölnir.

In the Eddas, Thor is married to the earth goddess Sif, who is known for her amazing golden hair. Wherever she walks, crops grow behind her. In *Gylfaginning* of the *Prose Edda*, it is revealed that she also had a son from a previous relationship, the handsome and all-round good guy Ullr, who is also a mighty warrior. She and Thor share a daughter named Thrúd ("strength"), who is likely a Valkyrie as that name is listed among them. It is widely held that there are missing myths about Thrúd, not least since the jötun Hrungnir is referred to as the "thief of Thrúd," but no story remains to explain it in any of the sources.

For the Vikings, Thor was the embodiment of thunder. The rumbling and crashing sounds were his chariot charging across the sky, while bolts of lightning were said to be his flashing hammer as he flings it far away to bring down the jötnar. Thor wears great iron gauntlets called Járngreipr, which help him to manage the immense power of Mjölnir, and his belt, Megingjörd, doubles his already legendary strength.

Thor drives a chariot pulled by two goats named Tanngrisnir ("teeth grinder") and Tanngnjóstr ("thin teeth"). In the *Prose Edda*, it is revealed that these goats also sustain the great god since they can be slaughtered each day. Thor then eats their meat. Provided the bones are left intact, Thor can resurrect them the following day using mystical powers from his hammer, Mjölnir.

In one myth, Thor and Loki stay the night with some peasants and share the goat meat with them. A boy, Thjalfi, breaks one of the leg bones to enjoy the marrow inside. The next morning, when the goats are brought to life again, Thor is angry to find that one of them is lame. When he finds out why, he takes Thjalfi and his sister, Röskva, to serve him. (In some translations, they are referred to as Thor's slave children.)

Thor noticing the lame leg of one of his goats.
https://commons.wikimedia.org/wiki/File:Tanngrisnir_and_Tanngnj%C3%B3str_by_Fr%C3%B8lich.jpg

The four leave the peasant's small holding and venture into the forests of Jötunheim. By nightfall, cold and tired, they find a large empty building and sleep inside. The next morning, they discover that it is actually a glove of the jötun giant Skrymir, who does not see them. The following night, they sleep in a nearby clearing, but Skrymir is sleeping nearby under a massive oak tree. His snoring is so loud that the earth shakes.

Thor, thinking the sleeping giant is vulnerable, takes Mjölnir and strikes Skrymir's head three times with all of his might. This appears to have little effect, but Skrymir awakens and, after stretching and opening his sleepy eyes, notices Thor. The god of thunder quickly has to think on his feet and asks the giant his name.

Once they have made their introductions, Skrymir tells them that he thinks some acorns and bits of foliage must have fallen during the night as he felt something drop on his head. He also warns the group that if they are heading for Útgarda-Loki's castle, they should modify their boastful and arrogant attitude.

Thor, Loki, and the children soon find themselves outside Útgarda-Loki's castle, a structure so immense they have to crane their necks to see its full height. The gate is closed, and Thor cannot pry it open, so they are forced to ignobly squeeze through the bars. They then find themselves in a great hall with giants seated on two benches. The ruler of the castle, Útgarda-Loki himself, eyes the group beadily.

He tells them that in order to enjoy his hospitality, they each have to perform a feat, with the exception of Röskva. Loki quickly volunteers to demonstrate his famous talent for eating. He is given a huge platter of food and competes against a giant named Logi, who eats far more quickly than the god of mischief, leaving the trickster god defeated.

Thjalfi declares that he is a fast runner, so a race is arranged between him and a diminutive man named Hugi. They race three times, with Hugi decidedly beating Thjalfi every time.

Finally, it is Thor's turn. First, he tries a drinking contest. Despite taking three colossal drafts, he is soundly beaten. Then, in a trial of strength, he finds himself unable to lift a large grey cat, only managing to raise one of its paws with a great deal of effort. Thor loses his temper and demands that he should wrestle one of the giants in the hall. None of them will fight, saying Thor is clearly an unworthy adversary. Útgarda-Loki calls for his nurse, Elli, a wizened old woman, to fight, and she and Thor begin to grapple. Again, Thor is hopelessly outclassed, and Elli brings him down. Afterward, Útgarda-Loki, as good as his word, gives them rooms for the night after they have eaten.

The next morning, the demoralized group is welcomed by their host, who asks them how they feel about the contests the night before. Thor tells him he cannot understand how he could have failed so badly and fears for his reputation. Útgarda-Loki reveals that he and Skrymir are one and the same and that all isn't as it seemed. The three blows that Thor had made to the giant's head while he was sleeping were so mighty that they had almost killed him and created great valleys in the landscape. In his contest, Loki had been pitted against a wildfire that quickly devoured all in its path. Thjalfi had raced against thought, and Thor had lowered the level of the sea with his drinking. The cat he had tried to lift was actually the serpent Jörmungandr. When he lifted its paw, he had actually held it up into the sky. The old woman Elli was, in fact, old age, something that no one can beat.

After telling them that they were actually formidable opponents, Útgarda-Loki says that he hopes they will not meet again. The furious Thor starts to swing his hammer, but the giant and the castle disappear.

In another myth, retold in both the *Poetic Edda* (*Hymiskvida*) and the *Prose Edda* (*Gylfaginning*), the sea god Ægir and his wife Rán plan a feast for the Æsir at their great hall underneath the waves. However, they need a cauldron big enough to prepare mead for all their invited guests. The god Tyr knows that the jötun Hymir has the largest, and Thor volunteers to go to Jötunheim in order to obtain this cauldron.

Hymir is not happy to see Thor since the god is a friend of Midgard. Nevertheless, he prepares for Thor's stay by slaughtering three bulls. By the first evening, Thor has already eaten two of them. The next day, Hymir, annoyed by his guest's ridiculous appetite, suggests a fishing trip and sends Thor to find some bait. Rather ungraciously, Thor returns with the head of the largest of Hymir's remaining bulls. Nevertheless, the two row out to sea. Hymir is delighted to catch two whales, but Thor seems nonplussed and starts to row the boat farther and farther out into deeper waters. Hymir protests, reminding Thor that it is the domain of the horrible serpent Jörmungandr, but Thor continues until he finally casts his line. Soon, it is clear that Thor has hooked the monster. Sea water begins to pour over them as it thrashes around on the end of Thor's line, and the boat threatens to fall apart.

Alarmed, Hymir shouts at Thor, telling him to let Jörmungandr go, but Thor, well aware his destiny is to fight it to the death, refuses and stands firm in the disintegrating boat. As the serpent's head emerges from the water, Thor takes his hammer to finish it off. Just as he is about to strike, the terrified Hymir cuts the line. Jörmungandr lives to fight another day. Thor is furious and, with a roar, throws Hymir overboard. He then returns to Asgard with the jötun's kettle and the two whales slung over his shoulder.

In the *Poetic Edda* (*Hymiskvida*), the story is similar, but at the point when Thor catches the serpent, volcanos erupt, and a great earthquake causes Thor to lose his grip. Jörmungandr slips back into the sea. Afterward, Hymir takes Thor back to his hall and challenges him to try and break his indestructible cup. Thor smashes it against his head and then quickly leaves with the cauldron while being pursued by giants.

In the prophecy of Ragnarök, Thor will battle Jörmungandr to the death, and in some ways, this myth whets the appetite for this great, final fight.

Before that terrible day, Thor has a particularly stressful adventure when his beloved hammer, Mjölnir, is stolen. Realizing it is missing, he calls upon Loki, telling him he suspects one of the jötnar has stolen it. Loki borrows Freyja's falcon feather cloak and flies over Jötunheim to the hall of Thrym.

The jötun readily admits stealing Mjölnir and tells Loki that the Æsir cannot hope to find it. He has buried it deep underground, but he will return it if Freyja becomes his wife.

Loki returns to find Thor waiting for him. When he learns of Thrym's demand, he tells Freyja that she should get ready for her wedding. Unsurprisingly, Freyja will have none of it and leaves the Æsir to sort out the dilemma themselves. Without Mjölnir, the citadel is far more vulnerable to attack from marauding jötnar.

Finally, Heimdallr suggests a crazy plan. Thor, whose stature is such that the rainbow bridge of Bifröst cannot support his weight, should dress as the lovely, willowy Freyja. With a veil, Thrym and the jötnar will be fooled. Thor is very reluctant to embrace his femininity, but he finally agrees when he realizes it is the only way he will be reunited with his hammer.

Dressed for marriage and wearing the precious necklace Brísingamen, Thor sets out with Loki beside him, who is dressed as his handmaiden. When Thrym sees he will have his "bride," he prepares a magnificent wedding feast that befits the great goddess Freyja.

An early 20th-century depiction of Thor dressed as Freyja.
https://commons.wikimedia.org/wiki/File:Ah,_what_a_lovely_maid_it_is!_by_Elmer_Boyd_Smith.jpg

The wedding party prepares to feast, and the veiled bride drinks an ocean of mead and consumes an entire ox before her betrothed has even started eating. Then, "she" devours eight sizeable salmon, one after the other, without pause, before eyeing some of the other delicacies.

Before Thrym grows too suspicious of his bride's astonishing appetite, Loki tells him that Freyja was so excited at the prospect of marrying him that she had been unable to eat for more than a week. This assuages Thrym's doubts for a while. The quick-thinking Loki is also able to explain Freyja's beard and angry, growling voice.

Boldly, the jötun leans over and lifts his bride's veil a little, revealing Thor's eyes that burn like fire. Alarmed, he turns to Loki, who explains that Freyja has also been unable to sleep in anticipation. By then, most of the jötnar wedding guests are growing uneasy.

One of Thrym's sisters asks the bride for a bridal token to seal their friendship, but the veiled bride stays silent and does not move. Thrym, anxious to please Freyja, demands that Mjölnir should be brought to the table so she can see he is honorable.

As soon as the hammer is within reach of Thor, he throws off his veil and swings Mjölnir, calling upon all of his power and might. With great claps of thunder and flashing bolts of lightning, Thor fells several jötnar and destroys the hall, with the burning roof and walls collapsing to crush the remaining guests as he and Loki depart in a cloud of thunder.

Thor fighting against giants.
https://commons.wikimedia.org/wiki/File:M%C3%A5rten_Eskil_Winge_-_Tor%27s_Fight_with_the_Giants_-_Google_Art_Project.jpg

Chapter Ten: Legendary Creatures from Norse Myths

The Norse realms are inhabited by creatures and entities that are much harder to identify with than the gods but still provide wonder and fascination. Some creatures are "fairer to look on than the sun," such as the Ljósálfar (light elves) of Álfheim, while others inspire fear, revulsion, and horror.[12]

Only the barest of details are known about the light elves, who are ruled over by Freyr. Regularly in the company of the Vanir and the Æsir, they appear to be made welcome amongst the gods and goddesses. There are elves enjoying Ægir's feast and then looking on aghast, presumably, at Loki's vicious and foul-mouthed flyting in *Lokasenna* in the *Poetic Edda*. Some later stories based on the myths suggest that Freyr and Freyja are elves and that Vanaheimr and Álfheim have become one and the same.

There is also the suggestion that light elves are the equivalent of angels. In the *Prose Edda*, it is revealed that there are other realms beyond the nine, but they are so remote and abstract that they are barely known to the wisest beings of the (known) Norse cosmos. One is Andlàngr, which shelters the souls of the dead after Ragnarök and is "south of and above this heaven of ours." Above this realm is Gimlé, and above that is Vidbláinn. The character High admits, "We believe it is only light-elves

---

[12] *The Prose Edda—Tales from Norse Mythology*. Translated by Jesse Byock. Snorri Sturluson. Penguin Classics, 2005.

who inhabit these places for the time being."[13]

Völündr, the master smith married to the Valkyrie Hervör, is identified as an elf, but his actions are somewhat vengeful and grisly for such an ethereal and virtuous being even considering the provocations he endured. In the *Poetic Edda*, in *Völundarkvitha*, he is revealed to have been captured by King Nithuth, who cuts his hamstrings to prevent him from escaping before setting him to work on the island of Sævarstod, where he will make precious trinkets. The story then becomes increasingly dark. When the king's sons visit his workshop, the elf promptly kills them. "The evil was open when in they looked; He smote off their heads, and their feet he hid."[14] He then makes chalices from their skulls for their father, jewels from their eyes for their mother, and brooches from their teeth for the king's daughter. He then rapes the king's daughter and leaves her pregnant with a son, Vidga (a character in several Scandinavian ballads). Völündr flies to the royal palace on mechanical golden wings he has fashioned (in some of the myths, he uses the swan cloak of his Valkyrie wife) to tell miserable King Nithuth what he has been up to. This myth, which has several variations, is known as Wayland the Smith in Old English and also appears in Old German, Old Frisian, and Old French traditional folk tales.

The light elves' cousins, the Dökkálfar, are represented in several myths in the Eddas, as well as sagas and folklore. Many of them are mentioned by name.

Skáldskaparmál in the *Prose Edda* talks about how Mjölnir is created. The god of mischief, Loki, finds Thor's wife, Sif, sleeping and thinks it will be a great joke to cut and steal her wonderful golden hair. When Thor returns to find Sif weeping, her head shorn, he is incensed with anger. When he catches up with Loki, he grabs him by the throat and shakes him like a rat.

Begging for mercy, Loki says he will get the dwarves to make Sif a crown of beautiful hair. It will be even better than the locks he had taken from her. Against his better judgment, Thor makes Loki swear to it and releases him. Thor loves his wife and cannot bear to see her so distressed.

---

[13] *The Prose Edda—Tales from Norse Mythology.* Translated by Jesse Byock. Snorri Sturluson. Penguin Classics, 2005.

[14] *The Poetic Edda.* Translated by Carolyne Larrington. Snorri Sturluson. Oxford University Press, 2014.

Loki goes to Svartálfheim and asks one of the dwarf craftsmen to make Sif a crown of golden hair that will magically attach itself to her head and grow like natural hair. He promises anything the dwarf asks in return.

The dwarf and his companions are delighted to have the opportunity to impress the gods. They state they will provide the lovely hair and two more gifts: a spear that will never miss its target and a ship that will always find a favorable breeze and can be folded up so that it can fit into its owner's pocket. Delighted, Loki takes these treasures to Asgard and insists that these dwarves cannot be matched for their craftsmanship to anyone who will listen.

A dwarf called Brokkr hears Loki's boasts and believes his brother, Sindre, can make even better items and tells him so. When he speaks up, Loki airily tells him that if he can make three better treasures, he can have his head!

Sindre begins to work on a pigskin that he throws in his furnace. Brokkr works the bellows to create the intense heat required for special enchantments. While he labors, a gadfly bites Brokkr's arm, but the dwarf resolutely continues to blow. Then, Sindre throws a golden ring on the fire. As Brokkr gets to work with the bellows again, the gadfly returns and bites his neck hard. Still, the dwarf takes no notice and continues his work.

Finally, Sindre puts an iron in the fire, and Brokkr determinedly takes up the bellows again. This time, the gadfly (which is often thought to be Loki in disguise) bites him between his eyes. This bite is so severe that Brokkr cannot see what he is doing. He stops working for a moment to brush the fly away.

Their work done, Brokkr takes their treasures to Asgard, where Thor, Odin, and Freyr have agreed to judge the contest. First, Loki gives Sif her crown of hair. She is delighted her beauty has returned. He then gives Odin the spear and Freyr the ship.

Brokkr gives Freyr a golden boar that is as fast as any horse. Its bristles shine so bright that they can make a dark night as light as day. He then gives Odin a gold armlet that will multiply into nine every ninth night. Each new armlet will be just as large and heavy as the first. Finally, he gives Thor the hammer Mjölnir and tells him it will never fail. No matter how far he throws the hammer, it will always return to him. Its only fault is the shortness of its handle, which had been caused by the momentary lapse while operating the bellows. Once Thor has tried the hammer, the gods agree that Brokkr and Sindre have won the contest.

Loki tries to escape, but Thor brings him back. Brokkr demands his prize: Loki's head. Eventually, Loki agrees that he will have to accede, but, with a flash of genius, he says he will not allow Brokkr to touch his neck (a story reminiscent of Shylock's bargain in Shakespeare's *The Merchant of Venice*). Brokkr was not altogether defeated. He took an awl and tightly sewed Loki's boastful lips together.

Brokkr and Sindre are much more reasonable and sympathetic characters than many of the dwarves in Norse mythology. Fáfnir was the son of Hreidmar, another dwarf, and had two brothers named Ótr and Regin. One day, Odin, Loki, and the god Hœnir were at the waterfall of Andvari, who was an incredibly wealthy dwarf who could turn himself into a pike at will.

When Loki spotted an otter, he killed it for its fur, not realizing it was the shapeshifting dwarf Ótr. As the gods continued, they came across Hreidmar's dwelling. They intended to sleep there, but as soon as their host saw Loki's otter pelt, he angrily demanded his son's blood-price (weregild).

Loki and Odin went back to the waterfall to find Andvari's treasure beneath the water. As they pulled up his mystical gold-finding ring and his Helm of Awe, Andvari watched, full of resentment, as he was powerless to stop the gods from taking his wealth. All he could do was curse the treasure, promising misfortune on anyone who possessed it.

The treasure is given to Hreidmar, and the gods continue on their way. However, Fáfnir is suddenly gripped by avarice. He kills his father, and to stop his surviving brother from getting his share, he takes Andvari's treasure into a forest cave and remains there, guarding it jealously.

As his hoard grows, thanks to the enchanted ring, Fáfnir's evilness catches up with him. He gradually transforms into a terrible dragon.

Regin, Hreidmar's remaining son, wants to avenge his father. He crafts a magical sword and gives it to Sigurd, the legendary Norse hero, who agrees to set out on a quest to slay the dragon.

Sigurd finds Fáfnir's cave and works out where he goes to take a drink. He digs a trench there, and the dragon soon falls into it. Sigurd slices its belly open with his sword. As he dies, Fáfnir warns Sigurd about the curse.

Regin asks Sigurd to remove the dragon's heart and roast it over a fire. As he attends to the flames, he burns a finger. When he puts the injured finger to his mouth, he ingests some of the dragon's blood. Immediately, he receives an incredible gift: he can understand the language of animals.

As Sigurd listens to the birds chattering, he learns that the treacherous Regin is planning to kill him so he can take the treasure for himself. Sigurd takes his sword and kills Regin as he sleeps and then eats Fáfnir's heart and drinks the other dwarf's blood for good measure. Then, having accrued greater wisdom and understanding, he leaves with Andvari's treasure.

In the *Skáldskaparmál* of the *Prose Edda*, which Snorri Sturluson based on the 10th-century Slavic poem *Haustlöng*, Thor agrees to a duel with the stone-headed (and stone-hearted) jötun Hrungnir. The jötnar are aware of Thor's prowess in battle, so they are uneasy at the prospect of this fight. Hrungnir's defeat would mean dishonor for them.

The jötnar decide to dredge the river at Grjotunagarder. They used the clay from the riverbed to build a massive giant. This giant is so large that his head is partly obscured by the clouds. The jötnar give their creation a mare's heart, and when it slowly comes to life, they name it Mist Calf (or Mökkurkálfi).

Thor and his servant Thjalfi arrive for the fight. Thjalfi fools Hrungnir into thinking that Thor is coming at him from underground. Hrungnir, armed with a whetstone, is then surprised by Thor's hammer, Mjölnir, flying toward him. Quickly, he flings his stone, but as the weapons make contact in mid-air, the hammer smashes the stone into tiny fragments that fly in all directions. The pieces that fall on Midgard formed whetstone quarries.

Mjölnir continues flying toward Hrungnir and strikes his stone head, crushing it. As he falls down, dead, Thor is trapped underneath one of the giant's huge legs. While Thor is stuck, Thjalfi attacks the giant's legs with his ax until the clay giant topples over, shaking the ground as he falls.

Eventually, Thor's son, Magni, lifts Hrungnir's leg, freeing Thor. However, Thor is left with a fragment of the whetstone stuck deep in his head, which causes him a lot of pain from time to time.

Other mythological creatures that may have been well known to the Vikings include Selkolla, a lovely young woman with the head of a seal. However, the earliest known account of this strange being is in the *Gudmundar Saga*, which recounts the life of Bishop Gudmundur Aragon (1161–1237). That is more than a century after the Viking Age came to an end. Similarly, Fossegrimen, a kind of water spirit, and huldra, forest sirens that lure young men into peril with their lovely voices or harp music, are considered part of Norse folklore but are not thought to have been popular during the Viking Age.

Chapter Eleven: Loki, the Trickster God, and the Beginning of the End

The most complex and contradictory of the Norse gods—if he is, in fact, a god at all—is Loki. Unlike the other deities, he has no clear area of responsibility, and there is no known hall in which he resides in Asgard, Vanaheimr, or Jötunheim. He is a wanderer with no fixed abode.

Loki has no known cults or worshipers amongst Viking or early Norse cultures. There is a possibility that Loki evolved through the ages and is actually derived from two entities: the trickster Loki of the Eddas and a "domestic spirit," or *vættr*, who lived under the fireplace and helped with farm work to bring wealth to the farm. This is thought to be the root of Loki's long-held association with fire, something that is not alluded to in the Eddas at all.

To add to the confusion, the traditional Norwegian folktale character Askeladden, "Ash Lad," is closely associated with Loki. They certainly share a similar intelligence and courage, but Askeladden is generally a neglected boy, forced to sleep in the ashes of the fireplace but goes on to achieves greatness, wealth, and status (much in the vein of the rags-to-riches Cinderella story). It is difficult to see much of the modern vision of Loki in the story of Askeladden.

Loki plays a role in almost each of the Viking myths. He is frequently presented as the Æsirs' problem solver. He often—but not always—arrives to alleviate situations that he has had a hand in. However, he is so much more than that. Loki is a shapeshifting clown, a trickster, a friend in need, a convenient scapegoat, and, as the stories draw to an end, a veritable demon. But prior to the Eddas, there is little evidence that Loki existed other than a few runestones that date from between 700 and 1000 CE that appear to depict scenes of myths in which Loki is a central character.

According to the *Gylfaginning* in the *Prose Edda*, Loki's father was the jötun Fárbauti ("cruel striker"), and his mother was the Æsir goddess Laufey ("leaves," or "foliage"), also known as Nál. He has two brothers, Byleistr and Helblindi. Other than their names, little is known of Loki's family.

From an early age, Loki aligned himself with his mother's race (this is made clear by his given name, Loki Laufeyson). In the *Lokasenna*, he reveals that he and Odin, who were both half jötun, at some time became blood brothers: "Remember, Odin, in olden days, that we both our blood have mixed." The two often travel together and seem to enjoy each other's company.

Although it is often argued that all of the Norse gods have flawed characters and indulge in decidedly unchivalrous and mean-spirited actions, Loki is something else. In the myths, he is portrayed as slippery, sly, scheming, cowardly, and reckless. Most of his schemes come to nothing, and he rarely ends with the upper hand for all his wily ways.

In a story that well illustrates his role in the myths, Loki, Odin, and Hœnir (one of the Æsir gods exchanged for Freyja, Freyr, and Njörd to settle the Æsir-Vanir War) are traveling in a remote, mountainous area. They are hungry and far from home when they come across a herd of oxen. The group decides to kill one of them to eat. But no matter how hard they try, the meat remains uncooked. The gods cannot understand how this can be until a large eagle perched in a nearby tree begins to speak to them. It reveals that it has enchanted the meat. If they promise to give him a share, he will release the ox from his spell. The gods agree, but once the dinner is ready, the eagle flies down and feasts on the best pieces of the meat. Annoyed, Loki takes a large stick and hits the eagle, but the giant bird clutches the stick in its talons and flies away with Loki still hanging onto it.

Loki shouts at the eagle, demanding to be set down. The great bird reveals himself to be Thjazi, the jötun sorcerer, and he makes Loki swear that he will bring him the goddess Idunn and her golden apples before setting him down.

After the three gods have returned to Asgard, Loki, mindful of the oath he had sworn to Thjazi, visits Idunn and tells her he discovered apples even more splendid than hers in a forest outside the fortified walls of Asgard. Curious, Idunn goes with him to compare them to hers, but Thjazi, in his eagle guise, is waiting and flies away with her.

Without Idunn and her marvelous fruit, the gods and goddesses soon begin to age. Greying, wrinkled, and increasingly infirm, they meet to find out where she has gone. Once they have ascertained that she was last seen leaving Asgard with Loki, they seize him and demand he should return her at once, or he will be killed.

Freyja lends him her magical hawk feather cloak, enabling him to shapeshift into a bird of prey. Loki flies off to Thrymheim ("thunder home"), Thjazi's great hall in Jötunheim. When Loki arrives, Idunn is all alone since her abductor is out fishing. Quickly, Loki turns her into a nut and carries her away as a hawk. However, Thjazi quickly gives chase when he returns to find Idunn missing. Loki arrives safely at Asgard and restores Idunn and her apples to the gods. He then organizes the building of a great fire in the realm's vast courtyard. Its flames set Thjazi's eagle feathers on fire. As Thjazi falls to the ground, the gods surround him, and he is killed.

Loki's antics often provide an element of comedy. Despite his propensity to trick and scheme, he is rarely the benefactor. For the most part, he is called on by the gods to right a wrong or alleviate a situation that is not necessarily of his own making.

In a vague passage in the *Poetic Edda*'s *Völuspá*, Loki's darker traits are explained by his eating some of a half-cooked heart (sometimes said to have been the Vanir goddess Gullveig at the time of her torture at the hands of the Æsir). This heart contained the soul of an "evil woman and resulted in him giving birth to three monsters: the goddess Hel, the wolf Fenrir, and the horrible serpent Jörmungandr. In other stories, these children were born from a relationship with the jötun Angrboda ("foreboding"), known as the "hag of the woods." Loki also had a family with his devoted wife Sigyn ("victory giver") and had one (or two) sons with her, Váli and/or Narfi.

In the myth of Baldr and Hodr, the sons of Odin and Frigg, we can see the evolution of the lord of mischief. He goes from a god who is always ready to help the gods when required with his tricksy, unconventional ideas and quick wits to a really unpleasant, sinister, and vicious character.

Baldr, the son of Odin and Frigg, was the god of light, joy, and summertime. He was loved by everyone, not just for his beauty and goodness but also for his wisdom, particularly for his talent for arbitration. He settled many arguments and disputes in Asgard and Midgard.

One night, Baldr and his mother dream the same vision that foretells his death. When Frigg tells Odin, he makes haste to Hel to find out if it is a prophecy. There, he finds a dead völva whom he resurrects. Although she is decidedly grumpy to be awoken from her final rest, Odin asks her to use her gifts to see into the future. She tells him that Baldr will die and that all of Asgard will mourn him.

When Odin tells Frigg what he has learned, she is determined that her glorious son will not die. She makes everything swear not to harm him; "fire and water ... likewise iron and metal of all kinds, stones, earth, trees, sicknesses, beasts, birds, venom, serpents."[15] Baldr was safe, or so everyone believed. Since they are so sure, it becomes a regular game to throw spears and weapons at him. They feel safe in the knowledge that he will be unharmed.

However, Loki feels irritated by Baldr's immunity to harm. He shapeshifts into an old woman and asks Frigg if it is true that she really convinced every single thing to take her oath. She concedes that she didn't bother with the humble mistletoe since it was so young.

The god of mischief scuttles off to find a sprig and makes it into a dart. When he finds the gods making their usual sport and Baldr enjoying the fun, he gives the mistletoe to Baldr's brother, the blind Hodr, and encourages him to join in. Loki even guides his arm so the dart finds its target. Hodr mortally wounds poor Baldr. As he lies dying, Odin whispers into his son's ear. These words, though important, have been lost, but the act itself is referred to in the Eddas (such as in *Gylfaginning* of the *Prose Edda*). It is generally presumed that Odin told Baldr that he would survive Ragnarök.

---

[15] *The Prose Edda—Tales from Norse Mythology.* Translated by Jesse Byock. Snorri Sturluson. Penguin Classics, 2005.

The death of Baldr.
https://commons.wikimedia.org/wiki/File:Baldr_dead_by_Eckersberg.jpg

Frigg, almost mad with grief, asks for someone to go and beg Hel to release her son. Hermod, Baldr's brother, takes Odin's horse, Sleipnir, to ride on for the long journey to Helheim. He finds Baldr there, lonely and miserable, and entreats Hel to release him as he had promised Frigg. He tells her that Baldr is the most beloved of all the gods and that everything is mourning for his loss. Hel agrees to release him on the condition that everything must weep for him first.

Everything does weep: gods, humans, animals, plants, and even stones cry out in grief. All that is except for an old giantess named Thökk, who is Loki in disguise. This giantess just sits in her cave and refuses to weep. Devastated, the Æsir are forced to accept that Baldr is lost to them. His body and Nanna, his wife, are placed on his ship, *Hringhorni*, which is then set ablaze at sea. This rite is commonly associated with the Viking tradition but likely didn't take place, at least not on the scale most people assume.

Odin wants to punish the killer of his dead son. He has two sons with the giantess Rindr. In a particularly unpleasant account in the *Gesta Danorum*, written by Saxo Grammaticus in the 13th century, Odin makes her mad and then rapes her. These sons, Vídar, the silent god of vengeance, and Váli, the god of revenge, reach maturity in a day. Váli kills his half-brother, the blind Hodr, just as he had been born to do.

According to *Lokasenna* ("The Flyting of Loki") in the *Poetic Edda*, Loki becomes infinitely more malevolent and unpleasant after Baldr's death. As the gods gather at the island of Hlesey in the hall of Ægir, the hospitable sea god, Loki takes one of his host's servants and kills him. Outraged, the gods throw Loki out. After licking his wounds in the forest, he barges back into the hall where the gods and goddesses have resumed their feasting.

The assembled gods are appalled, but Odin insists Loki should be allowed to sit. He warns the trickster god to behave. Loki is having none of it, though. He accuses the god Bragi of being a coward and his wife, Idunn, who is trying to prevent him from reacting, of being wanton and sleeping with her brother's murderer.

Loki then turns on Odin. He mocks Odin's interest in *seidhr* as being unmanly and compares him to a witch. Odin dryly points out that he is not the one who has born several children. Frigg tries to calm the situation by suggesting they should forget the past and move on. Loki has other ideas and accuses her of being a whore and sleeping with Odin's brothers while Odin was away.

Eventually, Loki makes the fatal mistake of revealing that he was behind Baldr's death. Freyja, furious, tells him that Frigg already knows that even if she has not said it, whereupon Loki accuses her of sleeping with every god and elf in the hall. When she tells him he is lying and warns him that he will regret his words, he accuses her of sleeping with her brother.

Njörd, Freyja's father, does not improve matters. After suggesting that it does not really matter who sleeps with whom, married or not, he trades insults with Loki. The god of mischief makes further claims about incestuous relationships between the Vanir deities, which are not denied. At this point, the god Tyr points out that the Vanir god Freyr is "the noblest of all the brave gods," but Loki rounds on him and reminds him that he lost his hand to Fenrir, Loki's son.

Freyr speaks up for Tyr and is insulted. Next, Loki tears into Freyr's servant, then Heimdallr, and then Skadi, who tells him, "You won't be at large, twirling your tail, much longer. The gods will bind you to a boulder with the guts ripped out of your ice-cold son." Loki fires back that he led the party that captured and killed her father, the jötun Thjazi.

Sif, Thor's wife, attempts to calm the situation, protesting that she is "wholly guiltless," but Loki counters that he has enjoyed a night with her. Turning to Freyr's other servants, he makes some particularly vile and xenophobic remarks as Thor enters, raging, having heard some of what Loki has had to say.

Thor threatens Loki, who, in turn, calls him "the son of the earth," Loki reminds him of some of his more embarrassing escapades (namely his failures in the jötun Útgarda-Loki's hall) and mockingly reminds him of the prophecy and the end of the Æsir. Loki finishes by ominously telling the gods and goddesses that this will be their last feast and then walks out, leaving them (presumably) shaken and appalled.

Loki is well aware that he has gone too far, but there is no going back, not least because he has publicly revealed that he was responsible for Baldr's death. He flees to a remote area in the far reaches of Asgard, where he builds himself a hidden cabin with several doors from which he can watch and easily escape if his enemies approach.

Paranoid, anxious, and worried the Æsir will catch up with him, Loki often leaves his home in the form of a salmon. He leaps into the boiling waters at Franang's Falls, but he still does not feel safe and returns to his cabin.

The next day, as Loki sits by his fire, fretting and wondering what to do, he anxiously knots together some lengths of twine and soon arranges them in such a way that he finds he has inadvertently constructed a fine net.

At the same time, Odin has found Loki from his throne, Hlidskjalf, high above Asgard. A group of gods sets out to capture him. As they draw near, Loki hears them. He throws his net into the fire and runs for Franang's Falls, where he becomes a salmon once more.

The party of gods enters Loki's cabin and finds it empty. But when they notice the ashes from the net Loki had made and realize it is some device for catching fish, they sit in the cabin, painstakingly recreating it. Once it is complete, they take it to the falls where Loki, as a salmon, is hiding. Thor casts the net into the water. Loki manages to avoid capture during the first two attempts, but on the third, he is caught in the net. He tries to jump away, but Thor grabs him and holds him tight. There is no escape this time.

Some of the gods take Loki to a dark cave, while the others go after Loki's sons, Váli and Narfi. They turn Váli into a wolf, and he immediately turns on his brother and tears him apart before turning tail and bounding away in the direction of Jötunheim. The gods remove poor Narfi's entrails and take them to the cave where Loki is lying, no longer a fish. He refuses to look at any of them or even speak. Then, the gods take their revenge. They tie him to a great slab of stone with Narfi's entrails that become as hard as iron once he has been restrained. Loki's wife, Skadi, brings a horrible snake, which is fastened over him in such a way that its poison will drip onto his face.

And there Loki remains, just as Skadi said, bound and helpless in a dark, damp cave. However, Loki is not alone. Skadi chooses to remain with him, devotedly holding a wooden dish above his head to catch the dripping snake venom. When it is full, and she leaves to empty it, the snake's poison that drops onto Loki's face makes him struggle so much that it causes the earth to tremble.

THE PUNISHMENT OF LOKI.

The punishment of Loki.
https://commons.wikimedia.org/wiki/File:Louis_Huard_-_The_Punishment_of_Loki.jpg

Chapter Twelve: Ragnarök, Twilight of the Gods

"The sun turns black, earth sinks in the sea,
The hot stars down, from heaven are whirled;
Fierce grows the stream, and the life-feeding flame
Till fire leaps high, about heaven itself."
Völuspá, the *Poetic Edda*[16]

The end of the world, Ragnarök, is foretold in the Eddas. Uncharacteristically, the *Poetic Edda* and the *Prose Edda* are, more or less, in accord regarding the details of this Viking Armageddon.

It begins with the most bitter winters: three consecutive years of biting winds, ice, and snow. Nothing can grow, there is no food to be found, and civilized beings revert to savagery to survive. Fathers kill their sons, brothers slaughter brothers, and civilized society will be forgotten in a bizarre orgy of incest. "An axe age, a sword age, a wind age, a wolf age," the völva summarizes for Odin in *Völuspá* as she describes the prelude to the great battle.[17]

---

[16] *The Poetic Edda*. Translated by Carolyne Larrington. Snorri Sturluson. Oxford University Press, 2014.

[17] *The Poetic Edda*. Translated by Carolyne Larrington. Snorri Sturluson. Oxford University Press, 2014.

The advent of the battle itself is heralded by Sköll and Hati, huge, hungry sky wolves who have been hunting the sun and the moon since their creation. They finally manage to catch and devour their prey with all the bloodshed and gore expected of such a demise. The skies are left dark and empty.

In this ominous prelude to the end, the Norns are fully occupied, busily weaving the strands of fate and deciding the destinies of the gods, jötnar, and humankind.

The world tree Yggdrasil starts to tremble, which causes the chains that hold the fearsome wolf Fenrir, who is in a state of frenzied rage after having been tricked and held captive for so long, to bend and break. Loki's other monstrous offspring, the colossal serpent Jörmungandr, rises from the sea. His frenzied writhing causes the horrible, ghostly ship *Naglfar* (made from the fingernails and toenails of dead men and women) to break its moorings and set sail for Vígrídr ("plain where the battle surges"), where the final conflict, according to the prophecy, will take place. *Naglfar*, which is sometimes said to be captained by Loki, carries the ice giant Hrym and his people. The ship will serve as a ferry to carry the frost giants to war.

Odin will understand that the day of Ragnarök has arrived after consulting the severed head of Mímir. He will then open the gates of Valhalla, and his army, the *einherjar*, armed and prepared, will march on Vígrídr. It is a field "a hundred leagues long and just as wide," according to *Vafþrúðnir* in the *Poetic Edda*. Odin leads them, along with the gods of the Æsir and Vanir.

At the same time, the sky will splinter and crack, allowing the fire giant Surtr-holding aloft his sword that gleams brighter than the sun-to lead the demons or fire giants from Muspelheim. They will storm over the rainbow bridge Bifröst, which crumbles away as they pass, alerting Heimdallr, the watchman of the gods. Heimdallr will blow Gjallarhorn, the enchanted horn that could be heard throughout all of the realms, calling everyone to war.

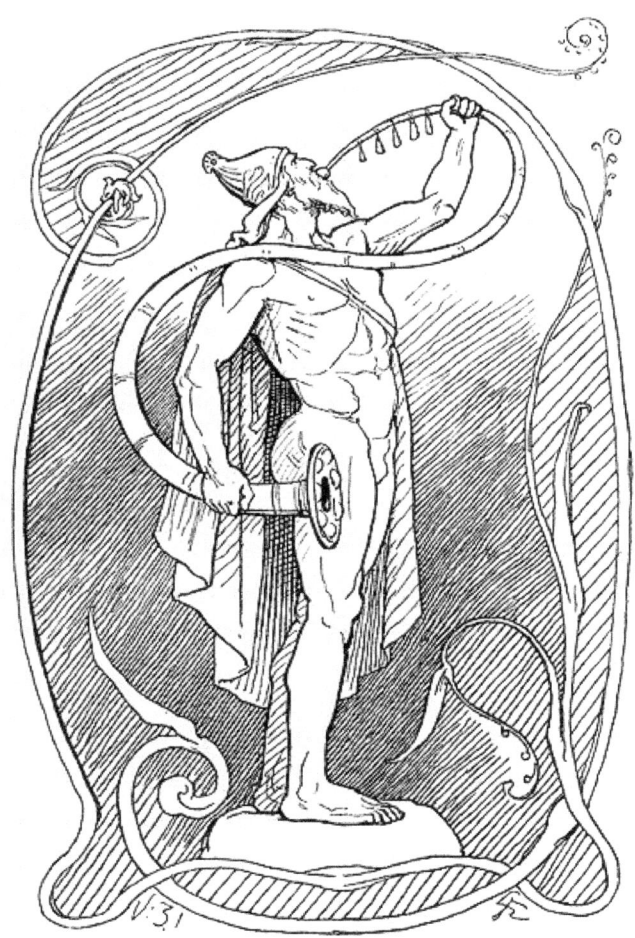

A 19th-century depiction of Heimdallr blowing Gjallarhorn.
https://commons.wikimedia.org/wiki/File:Heimdallr_by_Froelich.jpg

As Mímir's head falls to the ground, the *Völuspá* refers to Yggdrasil for the last time:

> "Yggdrasil shivers,
> the ash, as it stands.
> The old tree groans,
> and the giant slips free."[18]

---

[18] *The Poetic Edda*. Translated by Carolyne Larrington. Snorri Sturluson. Oxford University Press, 2014.

The final battle begins. The *einherjar* fight valiantly, just as they had practiced during their long stay at Valhalla. Fenrir approaches Odin, fire blazing from his eyes and nostrils. After a mighty battle, Fenrir devours his enemy. Odin's son, Vídar, the silent god of vengeance, exacts the revenge he was born for. He wears a shoe made from all of the leather ever discarded by the cobblers of Midgard. According to the *Gylfaginning* in the *Prose Edda*, he stamps on Fenrir's lower jaw and then grabs his upper jaw with one hand. With his other hand, Vídar drives his sword deep into the beast's throat, killing him.

Thor takes on his old enemy, the serpent Jörmungandr. After a grueling fight, Thor staggers back, victorious, but after taking nine steps, he, too, is dead, having ingested too much venom.

White and shining Heimdallr battles Loki, who has escaped his bonds. They kill one another. The powerful god of war, Tyr, wrestles the hellhound Garmr. (In the *Poetic Edda* poem *Völuspá*, his howls from Hel warn of the coming of Ragnarök.) They are both killed.

The Vanir god Freyr faces Surtr, but since he no longer has a weapon, having given his sword away during his courtship of Gerd, it is hopeless. Tyr is quickly slain.

With all the old gods defeated, Surtr raises his sword, and the realms sink beneath the sea, leaving a great void of nothingness. It is the end.

Time passes. Sól (or Alfrödull) had a daughter immediately before she was devoured by Sköll. The new Sól (as she was named) is just as beautiful as her mother and takes the reins of the chariot her mother once guided through the skies.

A new world begins to evolve. On the field of Iðavöllr ("splendor plain"), where the city of Asgard had previously been, the surviving gods assemble. Odin's sons Baldr and Hodr appear, as do their half-brothers Vídar and Váli, the latter having survived Ragnarök. Thor's sons, Magni and Mödi, are also there with Thor's hammer, Mjölnir. Presumably, there are also other goddesses and gods who survive, but they are not named in the Eddas.

These new gods set about creating a new world for themselves. "Shrines and temples they timbered high; Forges they set, and they smithies ore, tongs they wrought and tools they fashioned."[19] They build

---

[19] *The Poetic Edda.* Translated by Carolyne Larrington. Snorri Sturluson. Oxford University Press, 2014.

the shining city of Gimlé and live in a hall with a gleaming, golden roof.

As for humankind, a man named Líf ("life") and a woman named Lífprasir ("life of the body") manage to survive. They had concealed themselves in a wood (or tree) called Hoddmímis holt. As the worlds are reborn, they are sustained by the morning dew and worship Baldr. Because of them and their children, the world will be repopulated again.

> "Now do I see, the earth anew
> Rise all green, from the waves again;
> The cataracts fall, and the eagle flies,
> And fish he catches, beneath the cliffs."
>
> *Völuspá*, the *Poetic Edda*[20]

---

[20] *The Poetic Edda.* Translated by Carolyne Larrington. Snorri Sturluson. Oxford University Press, 2014.

Conclusion

Few cultures continue to fascinate us like the Vikings, and the popularity of the Norse myths continues to endure.

The larger-than-life characters, their relatable qualities, and the fantastical worlds in which they exist have an irresistible appeal that has captured the imagination of writers, artists, composers, and performers through the centuries.

Shakespeare was influenced by Norse mythology. The witches in *Macbeth* could easily be Norns, and some of the relationships, particularly those between Loki and the other gods, are echoed in his plays. *Hamlet*, arguably Shakespeare's most powerful work, deals with revenge and moral corruption and is based on the ancient story of Amleth, the story of the Viking King Rorik's grandson. In the legend, jealous Feng slays his brother to marry Gerutha (Amleth's mother), and Amleth pretends to be mad to save himself from Feng's malicious intent. Feng sends his witless stepson to England with two of his men and a letter ordering his execution, but Amleth alters it so that it is an order for his escorts to be killed and for himself to be married to the king's daughter. Afterward, he returns to Jutland, where he finds Feng feasting with his nobles. Amleth burns the great hall and slays Feng to avenge his father. As the Eddas were not translated during his lifetime, Shakespeare became familiar with the stories from oral traditions or from long-lost accounts or plays.

The 19th-century composer Richard Wagner immersed himself in the *Poetic Edda* and *Prose Edda*, believing medieval culture held profound truths that might help explain the meaning of life. His operas, such as *Das*

Rheingold, which tells the story of Andvari, the dwarf who forged a magic ring that was stolen by Odin (Wotan) to pay for the building of Valhalla, reflect his fascination with the subject.

J. R. R. Tolkien's *Lord of the Rings* is steeped in reimagined Viking mythology. For example, there is the use of runes and the various lands that compare to the realms of Midgard, Álfheim, and Svartálfheim. Tolkien interwove his lands and their inhabitants with real places and people. His central character, Gandalf, is often compared to Odin.

The mysterious, illusive, all-knowing, and bearded character with a whiff of sorcery, the All-Father, Odin, is a mainstay of fantasy and science fiction. This character offers protection and guidance to the good. His reflection can be seen in the *Star Wars* movies as Obi-Wan Kenobi and in the *Harry Potter* franchise as Professor Dumbledore. Dumbledore, just like Odin, has the thorny problems of prophecy to deal with.

In children's literature, the *Chronicles of Narnia* have more than a sprinkling of Christianized Viking mythology (Aslan's ancestor was Balder the Beautiful). The charming, award-winning animated show and books of the friendly Viking Noggin the Nog delighted and informed little ones in the last century. Players of the role-playing game *Dungeons & Dragons* are likely all too familiar with the various creatures and entities the Vikings revered.

More recently, Thor and Loki have captured the hearts and minds of a whole new audience with the Marvel comics, games, and blockbuster movies dedicated to the adventures of Thor and Loki. These battle-hardened warriors would surely appeal to the Scandinavian cultures from where they originated.

But for the Vikings and their forefathers, when life was hard and bewildering, stories of the nine realms, the gods, goddesses, and other beings, and the creation of the cosmos and its ultimate destruction helped them make sense of the world around them. The cycle of life and the inevitability of death, upon which the myths are framed, were concepts they were well used to. However, with the myths, they were better able to accept the chaos and unexplained.

The myths are so much more than interesting stories. They were cautionary tales that warned about the consequences of bad behavior, and they gave impressionable young Norsemen and women aspirational heroes. They provided gruesome horror stories to thrill and frighten, comedies to amuse and delight, and romances with beautiful characters overcoming the odds for their happy endings.

There cannot be many who have read or listened to Viking myths and legends without imagining old and wizened Norse elders huddled around a warm fire in the dark midwinter months with their extended families and telling the stories that they had learned as children with great relish and drama. Imagine the wide eyes of little ones, delighting in the adventures of Odin, the Æsir, and the Vanir, jeering as murderous dwarves get their comeuppance, and clinging to their mothers at the mention of Jörmungandr and Fenrir.

Through these extraordinary and complex stories, we can connect with the past and our ancestors. Although the Vikings are in the past, we can still celebrate this gift that will continue to endure.

Part 2: Vikings in England

An Enthralling Guide to the Great Heathen Army and the Viking Raids, Wars, and Settlement in Britain

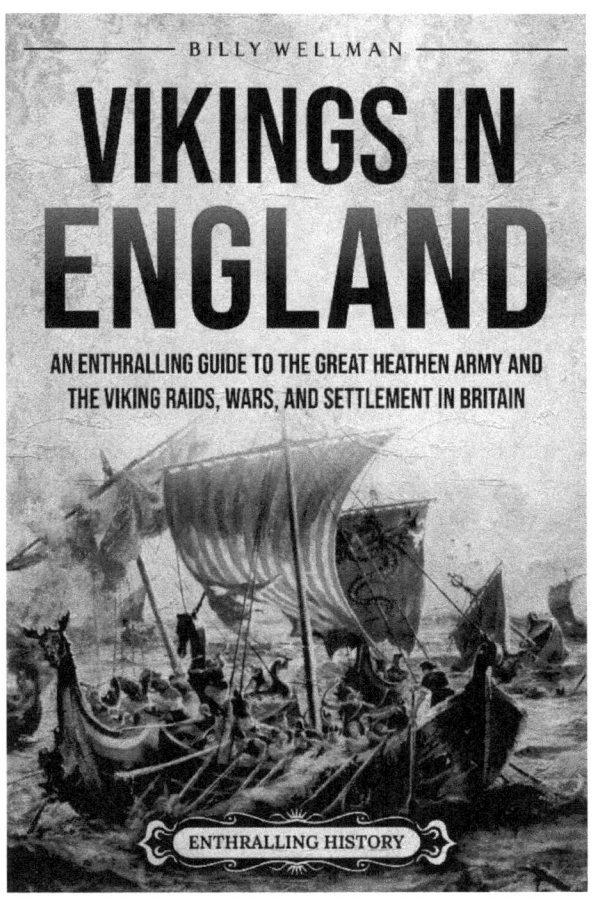

Introduction

Once upon a time, many years ago, a group of bearded men decided to go on an adventure that would allow them to visit a distant land and make a profit. They hopped in a boat with a dragon's head and rode out to the open sea, where they unfurled their sails and set off. A week or so later, they sighted land, hopped off their boat, and proceeded to burn, pillage, and rape their way through the community before they got back on their ship. This is not a Grimm Brothers' fairy tale or some myth from ancient sagas. This episode happened repeatedly in England during the Middle Ages. Those bearded men were not Santa or his helpers either; they were Vikings, and they were people that you did not want to play around with.

The Vikings were notorious pirates in the Middle Ages. People were in fear of them and what they were capable of doing. However, we must remember that much of what we once knew about the Vikings came from clergymen who were victims of Viking assaults. They portrayed the Vikings as senseless brutes. Fortunately, considerable research has diminished the monastic disinformation campaign, and we have a clearer picture of who these men were.

England was a principal target for Viking raids, and the Vikings created a great deal of disruption. However, these terrors of the high seas were markedly different from earlier sea raiders. Unlike the Sea People of the Bronze Age, Vikings made significant contributions to England's culture and language. They were also prominent in the commerce of the time period. The picture we now have of them is very different from what the monks once portrayed in their manuscripts.

In this book, we will be exploring the Vikings and their impact on England. We will be looking at who the Vikings were, why they chose England as a place to attack, their impact on the politics of the time, and what contributions they made to English society. Make no mistake; we admit that the Vikings caused a great deal of damage. However, an objective observer must admit that the sea rovers left a legacy behind that enriched England and other areas where they settled.

The Vikings' story is a fascinating tale comprised of facts and legends in equal measure. Understanding their deeds and their legacies enables us to gain a deeper appreciation of the forces that shaped medieval society. We can also gain greater insights into how the English language developed and how some of the legal and commercial customs we take for granted were initiated. The Vikings created more than they ever destroyed.

Chapter One: The First Viking Raids (780–850 CE)

The Vikings are often portrayed as ruthless warriors who terrorized Europe in the early medieval period. Although the Vikings are known for their many conquests, the Viking raids on England stand out for their ferocity and impact on English history. From 780 to 850 CE, Vikings made numerous incursions into England, raiding monasteries, towns, and cities, eventually establishing their own kingdoms. These events played a crucial role in shaping the history of England and the Viking Age.

The Doom Carrier: The Viking Drakkar

The Vikings relied on surprise and speed to be successful. A raid was a rather simple affair; they determined a target, landed close to it, attacked, pillaged, and then left as fast as possible. Typically, the Vikings came and went before any relief force was able to assist the region being attacked.

The greatest asset that the Vikings possessed was the ships on which they sailed. These were capable of outrunning any vessel the British kings had. What the Vikings designed were the most innovative boats of the Middle Ages.

And it was not just one particular craft. The Vikings had different types of longships. Let's look at a few of them:

- Karvi

The karvi was a smaller longship and could be used as a trade and transportation vessel. The karvi was equipped with thirteen rowing benches. Because it could handle shallow waters, it was ideal for transport and cargo. The best example we have of a karvi longship is the Gokstad ship. Discovered in 1880, it measures over twenty-three meters (a little over seventy-eight feet) in length.

- Snekkja

The English translation of snekkja is "snake," and that was how quick it was in the water. It had a minimum of twenty rowing benches and could carry a rowing crew of forty men. The standard snekkja was approximately seventeen meters (about fifty-five feet) long. It was a boat that was perfect for Atlantic expeditions. The snekkja was able to handle stormy weather and rough seas, which was essential for any journey across the North Atlantic.

- Skeid

The skeid was one of the larger Viking vessels. It was a warship that had thirty or more rowing benches. A skeid was excavated in the late 20th century that measured 37 meters (over 121 feet) long.

- Drakkar

The drakkar is the classic dragon ship of the Vikings. It stands out because of its elaborate carvings and the dragon head that is positioned on the bow. These ships were constructed to have thirty or more rowing benches.[21]

Design

The Viking longship was narrow and light, with a shallow draft designed specifically for speed. That shallow draft permitted navigation in water that could be as shallow as one meter. The design of the boat permitted beach landings, and its light weight allowed it to be carried over portages. An important feature of the longship was its double-ended design. The symmetrical bow and stern allowed the ship to reverse direction quickly without having to turn around. This was useful in raids, but this design had safety in mind. The North Sea was full of ice floes and other types of ice that were hazardous to shipping. A Viking boat could back out and navigate without any trouble, unlike other sea vessels.

The longships were made from oak timbers, with the bow and stern rising three to four meters high. The hull was approximately five meters

---

[21] Discover Middle Ages. (2023, August 31). *Viking Ships*. Retrieved from Discovermiddleages.co.uk: https://www.discovermiddleages.co.uk/medieval-life/viking-ships.

wide. Amazingly, there were no standard blueprints for the longships. Instead, the shipbuilders would rely on previously built vessels. The ship was built from the keel up.

Keels and sterns were made first and then the strakes, which were lines of planks joined endwise from stern to stern. A common design was the clinker, which had each hull plank overlapping the next. When the planks reached the desired height, the shipbuilders added an interior frame and crossbeams. The keel was narrow and deep, which provided strength beneath the water line. Waterproofing was done with animal hair, wool, hemp, or moss that was drenched in pine tar.

The sails were made from rough wool cloth and held in place by a mast that was up to sixteen meters tall. A side rudder was used to steer the boat. The average speed of these ships was from five to ten knots; the maximum speed in fair weather was approximately fifteen knots. Not only could a Viking ship sail safely across treacherous waters to get to its destination, but it could also outrun any vessel seeking to attack it.

Construction of a skeid longship.
Marit Synnøve Vea, CC BY-SA 3.0 <https://creativecommons.org/licenses/by-sa/3.0>, via Wikimedia Commons;
https://commons.wikimedia.org/wiki/File:DRAKEN_HARALD_H%C3%85REAGRE._9._BORD_GANG_SNART_P%C3%85_PLASS.jpg

Navigation

Vikings were able to cross vast stretches of ocean that did not have identifiable landmarks. Navigators would rely on experience, but there were some rudimentary navigation instruments that we believe the Vikings used to make their voyages successful.

Historians believe that Vikings used a sun compass. This instrument shows the correct direction and basically is a vertical pointer on a horizontal surface. The shadow of the pointer moves throughout the day. It forms a curve that is different at different latitudes and at different times of the year.

Problems arose on cloudy days. Vikings had to have some way of navigating when the weather was bad. Viking sagas speak of sunstones. These were minerals that could polarize light and determine the direction of the sun under cloud cover. To date, there has been no archaeological evidence of sunstones.[22]

Viking Weapons

Ragnar Lodbrok (more about him later) would have gone into battle equipped with some of the best weapons possible. What the local farmers or militia had was no match for what the Vikings carried as personal equipment. If one implement did not kill you, a Viking could easily use another to dispatch you.

A burial excavation at Woodstown, Ireland, gives us an understanding of Viking weaponry in the mid-9th century. The grave was of a warrior buried with all of his weapons. His personal arsenal included a sword, shield, spear, ax, and knife. These were the essential tools of war.

A man's sword took pride of place. These were treasured, and a man would pass down his sword to his son unless the sword was buried with a man. The blades were made of iron, meaning whoever had a sword was rich enough to afford the expense of creating it, although Vikings would also loot swords from the body of a dead enemy. The sword would be approximately ninety centimeters long and include a ten-centimeter tang, which was covered by the handle.

---

[22] Thomsen, M. H. (2023, August 10). *Instrument navigation in the Viking Age?* Retrieved from Vikingeskibs Muskeet: https://www.vikingeskibsmuseet.dk/en/professions/education/knowledge-of-sailing/instrument-navigation-in-the-viking-age.

The process for creating a Viking sword was nearly as elaborate as a Japanese samurai sword. Strips of wrought iron were welded together, twisted, and hammered out to shape the blade and given a hardened steel edge. Blades were tapered toward the point, and a blood groove was forged along the length. The swords were double-edged and were used for slashing. The Vikings even named their swords. Norse sagas mention blades called War-Snake, Viper, Dragon Slayer, and Widow-Maker.

Spears were standard. Because spears were easier to make, they are often found in large numbers at Viking burial sites. Spears were used for thrusting and throwing. The spears that were thrown would have small heads, while a broader, leaf-shaped head would be used as a stabbing weapon.

Axes had long handles. The ax heads had blades eight to sixteen centimeters long. They were elaborately decorated and permitted the warriors to have a long reach in battle. An experienced ax handler was a deadly force on the field.

Viking shields were nearly one meter wide with a central hole for an iron boss. An iron grip was attached to the boss on the inner face. These protective circles were decorated in bright colors and were the primary defense for Vikings.

Bow and arrows were used, but few fragments have been found so far. An arrow would be around fifteen centimeters long, and bows could be used for hunting as well as fighting.

Helmets were not the stuff of Wagnerian opera. No, Viking helmets did not have horns on the side. The Gjermundbu helmet, which was found in Norway, was an iron cap with four spokes and had a rim with a heavy eye and nose guard attached. Vikings did use chainmail, but this protective covering was very expensive to make. The nobility and elite warriors probably had chainmail, and some Vikings probably robbed corpses of their chainmail on the battlefield.

The Viking raids in England were characterized by their speed and the use of surprise tactics. In many cases, the Vikings would strike quickly, taking advantage of the element of surprise to catch their enemies off-guard. They would use the longship as a means of transport, attacking their targets along the coast and then sailing away before any resistance could be mounted. Their tactics were brutal, often involving the massacre of entire populations.

Perhaps the most famous Viking raid was when the Vikings attacked the monastery of Lindisfarne in 793 CE.

Lindisfarne

Monasteries in 7th-century England were places where men would gather in a communal society to worship and praise the Lord. They were places of extreme piety, and people would go there to renounce the world and seek the road to salvation, which was a major thought in most people's minds at the time. The nobility of the era sought to burnish their reputation by endowing monks with property, which the pious men used to build monasteries. King Oswald of Northumbria did this in 635 CE when he endowed an Irish monk named Aidan with a small island called Lindisfarne.

This speck of ground in the North Sea was six miles north of the Northumbrian capital of Bamburgh. The solitude that the monks looked for on Lindisfarne was enhanced by the causeway, which the tide covered twice each day, assuring a sense of isolation but also a connection to the mainland.

Lindisfarne's reputation was enhanced in the 670s when a monk named Cuthbert became part of the community. Cuthbert was a saint of early England and became the bishop of Lindisfarne. He became well connected to the Northumbrian court and was generally liked by everybody. His death caused Lindisfarne to be a pilgrimage site, as a cult grew up around his holiness. That brought dramatic changes to the secluded community.

After Lindisfarne became a major pilgrimage site in northeastern England, pilgrims went there to seek the aid and blessings of St. Cuthbert. They left behind more than just good wishes; many pilgrims made donations and left rich gifts to the monastery and its monks. Lindisfarne became important and rich. It had no fortifications, though, and the monks still led simple lives in the midst of great wealth. It had a reputation not only for sanctity but also for its treasures. Frankly, Lindisfarne was a pigeon waiting to be plucked. And that is what happened in 793.[23]

---

[23] English Heritage. (2023, August 10). *Early Christianity in Anglo-Saxon Northumbria.* Retrieved from English-heritage.org.uk: https://www.english-heritage.org.uk/visit/places/lindisfarne-priory/History/.

Viking Assault

This was not the first Viking raid on England. There was a smaller incursion a few years before in Wessex, and there is evidence of a raid in Kent around 753 CE. However, the raid on Lindisfarne was much more significant. The monastery was more than an isolated cloister. Lindisfarne had grown into an economic and political powerhouse in Northumbria. There were as many as four hundred people living on the island, which made it a huge community. The monastery had extensive landholdings. Moreover, the Vikings probably had a good idea of what Lindisfarne had as far as treasure. There is evidence that merchants from Scandinavia had been trading up and down the coast of Northumbria for years by 793.

The raid took place on June 8th, 793 CE. The *Anglo-Saxon Chronicle*, written sometime in the late 9th century, was succinct in its description: "The woeful inroads of heathen men destroyed God's church in Lindisfarne island by fierce robbery and slaughter."

That account would later be elaborated on by Symeon of Durham, whose account was a little more dramatic:

"They [the Vikings] miserably ravaged and pillaged everything. They trod the holy things under their polluted feet, they dug down the altars, and plundered all the treasures of the church. Some of the brethren they slew, some they carried off with them in chains, the greater number they stripped naked, insulted, and cast out of doors, and some they drowned in the sea."

The Shocking News

It was the reaction of the rest of Europe that made the raid on Lindisfarne so prominent. Charlemagne's court received the news, and Alcuin, Charlemagne's primary advisor, expressed genuine horror over what had happened.

The raid of Lindisfarne is considered the start of the Viking Age. Although the monastery survived for nearly one hundred years afterward, everything had changed. The entire coast of England was exposed to danger. Every monastery or undefended town was liable to be a victim of the Northmen.[24]

---

[24] Marsh, A. (2022, June 21). *In 793 AD, Vikings attacked Lindisfarne. Here's why it was so shocking.* Retrieved from National Geographic.co.uk: https://www.nationalgeographic.co.uk/history-and-civilisation/2022/06/in-793ad-vikings-attacked-lindisfarne-heres-why-it-was-so-shocking.

A Nasty Surprise

The attack on Lindisfarne was likely not a major assault; no more than four ships and a combined force of one hundred men attacked. The surprise factor was what gave the Vikings the advantage. Historians have suggested that the monks possibly did not know what was going on until they saw drawn swords. By then, it was too late to do anything but beg for mercy.

What makes the raid more shocking is that Scandinavian traders had been working up and down the coast and into the English Channel for years. There was no way to identify a trading ship from a Viking raider at that point, so no one could tell if the ship on the horizon was a Viking vessel. It came down to whom one could trust off the shores of England.

Prizes to Be Had

In any event, the Vikings began to target the wealthy monasteries along the coast. These English monasteries were rich in gold, silver, and other valuable goods, and they proved an irresistible target for the raiders. There would be an attack on the Benedictine abbey at Jarrow the following year and an assault on Iona the year after that. The assault on Jarrow was repulsed, but it did not stop later attacks on the monastery or on Lindisfarne.

The monks who lived in these monasteries were easy targets since they were not trained warriors. They had no weapons and no military training. The Vikings encountered little to no resistance from them, which led to further raids.

Something else was happening during all these incursions. Viking sailors were getting an idea of the lay of the land. They noticed the agricultural opportunities that were present in England. The raids were not just for the sake of gaining plunder; they were a chance to do some real estate hunting, which would prove valuable a few decades later.

In the Midst of Chaos

The attacks on the English coast might have had very different outcomes if a unified front and a strong coastal defense were present. Unfortunately for the English, that was not possible. What is now modern England was divided into four kingdoms in the 9th century: Northumbria, Mercia, Wessex, and East Anglia. Each had its own set of laws and political agendas. A Viking raid on Northumbria meant nothing to Mercia. In fact, such incursions would be desirable because they would distract Northumbria from trying to dominate other kingdoms.

The same is true for the other kingdoms. An attack on one was not necessarily an attack on all of them. However, the Vikings were not a menace that was going to go away. In fact, as the years progressed, the danger grew significantly worse with every passing year.

There was a serious dynastic rivalry in Northumbria between the royal houses of Deira and Bernicia. It created considerable dissension in England's largest kingdom. Between 737 and 806, Northumbria had ten kings. Five were expelled, three were murdered, and two retired to become monks. The raids on Northumbria's monasteries continued, and in 800, monasteries at Whitby, Tynemouth, and Hartlepool were assaulted. Northumbria's internal problems continued to make it vulnerable to outside attacks.

The developments in Northumbria were no doubt reported back to Scandinavia by traders who did business in England. We can think of them as industrial spies who saw opportunities developing thanks to inner chaos that prevented a strong resistance.[25]

Viking raids intensified in the 9th century. They were no longer small assaults but large-scale incursions. The distress spread to other parts of the island. The Vikings were defeated in 838 and in 851, but that did not stop raids in East Anglia, Kent (which became part of Wessex in 845), Wessex, and Northumbria.[26]

Just as a reminder, some of the accounts of the ferocious Vikings must be taken with a grain of salt. The stories of horror were penned by monks who had a revenge agenda. Their monasteries were burned, and their brother clergy were killed or dragged off to slavery. It is probable that tales of terror were deliberately exaggerated to make Vikings appear to be sons of Satan. They were rough sailors and not to be trifled with, but they most likely did not roast babies for dinner.

The Danes Are Coming!

The Vikings stopped concentrating on Northumbria and made attacks in southern England as well. Denmark was becoming the starting point for increasingly more incursions.

---

[25] England's North East. (203, August 10). *Northumbria's Downfall.* Retrieved from Englandsnortheast.co.uk: https://englandsnortheast.co.uk/northumbria-anarchy/.
[26] Dorothy Whitlock, W. A. (2023, August 10). *The Period of the Scandinavian Invasions.* Retrieved from Britannica.com: https://www.britannica.com/place/United-Kingdom/The-church-and-the-monastic-revival.

Plunder was not the only reason for Danish Vikings to have an interest in England. Danish society had a high regard for martial prowess and bravery. An ordinary warrior could gain a great deal of prestige and honor if he came back with considerable spoils. That man might even be named in one of the Viking sagas and oral traditions, guaranteeing that he would be remembered long after he was dead.

Denmark was also experiencing overpopulation. There was not enough arable land, and there were too many mouths to feed. The possibility of finding extensive tracts of farmland made England appealing as a place for future settlement.

Society in Denmark was full of feuds and duels fought because of honor. The chance to send aggressive men who could be troublemakers on long sea voyages would ensure that things remained quiet in the region as long as they were gone.

The slave trade needs to be thought of as a reason for striking England as well. Slavery was a part of Scandinavian culture, and victims of a Viking raid could be taken back as slaves. A chance to establish trade networks or take over existing ones was a possible reason as well.

The Danes would gradually become an even more potent force in English history as the Viking Age progressed. They were not in this enterprise to just gather up shiny bobbles and jewels.

Wintering in England

Early Viking raids were essentially grab-and-run affairs, but in 850, the *Anglo-Saxon Chronicle* had an interesting entry.

"In this year Ealdorman Ceorl with the contingent of the men of Devon fought against the heathen army at Wicganbeorg, and the English made a great slaughter there and had the victory. And for the first time, heathen men stayed through the winter on Thanet."[27]

This time, the Vikings were not racing home to celebrate or escape. They were wintering in a land they were accustomed to only plundering. The significance of this is subtle, but it is revealing. Vikings were developing an interest in England that went beyond making a quick profit. They were probably starting to consider the area as a possible place for settling down. Migration to England would certainly solve the

---

[27] History-maps.com. (2023, August 10). *Viking Invasions of England.* Retrieved from History-maps.com: https://history-maps.com/story/Viking-Invasions-of-England.

overpopulation problem back home. Many Vikings were farmers, not professional raiders.

Perhaps wintering in England was not out of necessity. The Vikings who stayed there had an opportunity to do some very detailed scouting and information gathering. The intelligence they brought back to Scandinavia would have influenced the decisions of very powerful men. The outcome of this stay would be realized several years later when the raids became something more than a plundering visit.

Primary Actors

The Viking Age provided history with a colorful cast of characters. Some of their exploits may appear a bit fanciful, but their individual contributions are too great to ignore. Here are some of the prominent players.

Famous Vikings

- Rollo of Normandy was so successful in his raids on France that he was finally given land at the mouth of the Seine in exchange for converting to Christianity and promising not to raid again. The land he ruled would become known as Normandy.
- Sweyn Forkbeard was, at one point, the king of England, Denmark, and parts of Norway. He will receive more attention later in this book.
- Gunnar Hamundarson was an Icelandic chief who was known for his fighting ability and athletic prowess. It was said that he was able to jump his own height!
- Erik the Red was another Icelander, and his claim to fame was discovering Greenland. Erik deliberately named the island to convince other Vikings to settle there.
- Leif Eriksson was the son of Erik the Red and was another Viking explorer. He is believed to be the first European to land on the shores of America.
- Cnut, also known as Canute, was the ruler of a great Viking empire. He receives individual attention in this book.[28]

---

[28] Warriors and Legends.com. (2023, August 31). *Famous Viking Warriors*. Retrieved from Warriorsandlegends.com: https://www.warriorsandlegends.com/viking-warriors/famous-viking-warriors/.

Famous Anglo-Saxons

The Kingdom of Wessex produced the most memorable Anglo-Saxons. They will receive attention later in this book.
- Alfred the Great
- Edward the Elder
- Æthelstan

Raids from Denmark were particularly marked from 835 CE onward. The Danish Vikings targeted Northumbria, the most powerful Anglo-Saxon kingdom at the time. They captured York twice in 866 and 873 CE and established their own kingdom there, known as the Kingdom of Jorvik. This kingdom was ruled by the famous Viking warrior Guthrum, who battled against the Anglo-Saxon king, Alfred the Great. Ultimately, however, Guthrum was defeated and forced to sign a peace treaty in 886 CE, which allowed the Vikings to retain control of the Kingdom of Jorvik but on English terms.

Chapter Two: Ragnar Lothbrok

The History Channel series *Vikings* features a notorious Viking named Ragnar Lothbrok (also spelled as Ragnar Lodbrok). According to Viking lore, Ragnar was the son of a hero, Sigurd Hring, and his wife, Alfhild. He was a man of legend and is credited with being a highly successful raider of England and other parts of Britain and perhaps even Ireland. His story is a combination of fact and fiction.

Viking oral histories and sagas are not always factually correct. They are often highly exaggerated accounts of the deeds of men, who are made to appear almost superhuman. One reason for this is that the storytellers were stressing the fame and power of the individual. Another problem is that hundreds of years often passed before the accounts were recorded. The primary source of information we have for Ragnar Lothbrok is the *Ragnarssona pattr* (the *Tale of Ragnar's Sons*). Other places where Ragnar is mentioned include *Gesta Danorum* (*Deeds of the Danes*), a Danish document that is reasonably accurate, and the *Anglo-Saxon Chronicle*.

It has been suggested that the accounts of Ragnar were deliberately exaggerated to make him look like a more significant threat than he actually was. The intent was to make him look so ferocious and terrifying that just mentioning his name could spread fear among his enemies.[29]

---

[29] Irvine, A. (2022, December). *10 Facts About Viking Warrior Ragnar Lodbrok*. Retrieved from Historyhit.com: https://www.historyhit.com/facts-about-viking-ragnar-lodbrok/.

His Raiding Resume

Vikings suggests that Ragnar led the raid on Lindisfarne in the 8th century. This is not true because Ragnar was not yet born when the attack happened.

Ragnar had a reputation for being a great warrior and became wealthy due to raids on vulnerable territories. Icelandic sources that have been somewhat verified by the Anglo-Saxons tell of a ferocious Viking named Ragnall who terrorized northeastern England. He might have been Ragnar.[30]

Viking lore implies that Ragnar attacked Paris around 845. It was assumed that he commanded a fleet of 120 Viking ships, which means that he went after Paris with six thousand men. That was a sizable army in those days.

A 19th-century depiction of Vikings attacking Paris.
https://commons.wikimedia.org/wiki/File:Viking_Siege_of_Paris.jpg

---

[30] The Ministry of History. (2020, May 5). *Ragnar Lothbrok*. Retrieved from Theministryofhistory.co.uk: https://www.theministryofhistory.co.uk/historical-biographies/ragnarlothbrok.

But was it even remotely possible that Ragnar could do this? Yes. There was also a later attack on Paris that took place in 885. This was the most significant Viking raid on the city. The initial estimate is that the Viking force had three hundred to seven hundred ships with anywhere from thirty thousand to forty thousand men. That estimate is a gross exaggeration. Historian John Norris estimates that the Viking force was around three hundred vessels, meaning the Viking army was approximately fifteen thousand men. That is still a significant army in the 9th century.

We need to keep in mind that this type of attack was possible thanks to the longships. Their shallow draft permitted them to go upriver instead of landing forces on the seashore. The sight of the Viking armada heading into the heart of France must have terrified everybody who saw it.

The attack of 885 was unsuccessful. Although the French were able to block the passage of the Viking ships down the Seine, the raiders were not deterred. The Vikings were able to retreat by dragging their boats overland to the Marne. Before they did that, the Vikings conducted a raid on Burgundy, which is even farther inland. The Vikings' ability to attack targets that were a considerable distance from the coast made people greatly fear them.

Legend has it that Charles the Fat paid a substantial bribe to Ragnar so that he would go away. Ragnar was only too happy to accept the money. Just attacking Paris gave him considerable prestige in the Viking world. Besides, there were other rich targets with weaker defenses. Saxo Grammaticus, a Danish historian who lived from around 1160 to 1220, tells us that Ragnar raided Ireland in 851 and continued his raiding along the Irish coast and northwestern England.[31]

Viking Raiding Tactics

Ragnar made use of a lightning strike tactic to overcome his victims. He demoralized and overwhelmed his opponent before they could gather enough strength to successfully oppose him. Ragnar was also a prudent general. He would fight when the odds were in his favor and would not take unnecessary risks.

---

[31] Butler, J. (2023, August 29). *The Real Ragnar Lothbrok*. Retrieved from Histori-uk.com: https://www.historic-uk.com/HistoryUK/HistoryofEngland/Ragnar-Lothbrok/#:~:text=This%20may%20well%20have%20been,settlement%20not%20far%20from%20Dublin.

Viking military strategy was very flexible. It all depended on the circumstances they were confronted with when they got off the boat. These men were out for loot, and they wanted to survive the raid. Vikings were quite willing to set up ambushes or engage in sneak attacks if it would help them gain their objective.

One very effective battle tactic the Vikings employed was the "boar's snout." It was meant to break the battle line of an enemy. A wedge of warriors was formed that would attack one part of the enemy line with the intention of breaching the defense. Once the line was broken, the Vikings would take advantage of the ensuing chaos.[32]

Ragnar's success stemmed from a society that nurtured a warrior spirit. Vikings were men who learned to fight early and had a cohesive spirit that encouraged group action. Making a Viking did not happen in a few weeks of basic training. It was a lifestyle born in childhood.

Grooming a Viking

Ragnar had several sons. Three of them, Halfdan, Ivar (known as Ivar the Boneless), and Ubba, would play significant roles in a massive Viking assault that happened in the late 9th century. Ragnar's sons were likely prepared for a life that would be part domestic work and violent action since they were boys.

When we say domestic work, we mean farming and crafts. Vikings were raiders, but Vikings only typically raided for a season. They would then come home to be farmers and craftsmen. A boy needed to learn how to excel in an occupation and be a skilled warrior.

History gives us detailed accounts of how the Spartans trained their boys to become exceptional fighters. We have no Viking training manual, but we can guess that boys learned what to do by working with their fathers and extended families. Uncles, grandfathers, and older brothers would be important teachers and mentors. Historians think that fighting was always part of a boy's training. If a boy was fighting another boy over a silly quarrel, the child was not punished severely unless serious physical harm happened.[33]

---

[32] Curry, A. (2017). *How to Fight Like a Viking*. Retrieved from Nationalgeographic.com: https://www.nationalgeographic.com/history/article/vikings-fight-warfare-battle-weapons.
[33] Legends and Chronicles. (2023, August 20). *Viking Children*. Retrieved from legendsandchronicles.com: https://www.legendsandchronicles.com/ancient-civilizations/the-vikings/viking-children/.

Viking sagas mentioned that boys were trained for war. The poem *Rigsthula* describes the education of a boy who could tame horses, shape shields, make arrows, and brandish spears. It is possible that toddlers learned how to play with wooden swords. There is evidence that children received real weapons that were suited to the size of the child. Archaeologists in Norway have found an ax and a sword in a minor's grave.

Wrestling was a popular sport in Viking culture, and it taught practical war skills, such as speed and agility. Snowball fights were opportunities to build snow forts and practice different throwing skills. Boys were allowed to play rough, but they were not permitted to hurt anybody. Breaking the rules in the wild and tumble games, committing what was called a *nio*, was a severe juvenile offense. (There is not enough evidence to know if girls were taught to fight, but it is a possibility.)

The Viking culture prized honor above other qualities. A code of honor was instilled into a young boy from the beginning. Bravery was an expected virtue that each boy needed to have because only a brave warrior would be permitted to enter Valhalla.

A grim part of the training was the battle itself. The sagas mentioned cases where a boy as young as nine killed a man. These may be exaggerations, but the understanding in Viking communities was very clear. A young man must be ready to enter battle for honor or pillage. There was no minimum age for combat.

Vikings as Fighters

Ragnar did not go a-roving with a band of amateurs. His crew was comprised of military-minded men who knew what they were doing. All accounts of Vikings from the sagas and the writings of monks indicate that these men were perhaps the best fighters of the Middle Ages. They had superior longships and excellent weapons, and they were trained from early childhood to be fighters. Some unique qualities of the Vikings made them nearly invincible.

- Esprit de Corps

Morale is essential for any fighting force, and raiding Vikings had high levels of confidence. An important reason for this esprit de corps, besides fighting for honor and loot, was the way the crews were comprised. The boat crews were formed from the men who came from the same village or local area. They knew each other from birth and were often relatives or close friends. A raiding expedition would be at sea for weeks to get to and from their destinations. The men got to know each other and developed strong connections.

The notion of a band of shield brothers was critical in a military engagement. No one wanted to look like a coward in front of their neighbors or relatives. Running from a battle would bring shame to a person, and that dishonor would last a lifetime. Like the legendary three hundred Spartans, Vikings would stand together and fight to the last man if necessary. Evidence from excavations of burial sites shows groups of Vikings buried together. It is likely they all fell fighting to defend each other.

- Berserkers

Berserkers are major characters in the stories of the Northmen. They were reportedly half-crazed wild men who would attack without concern for bodily harm and fought until they won or were killed. They were the insane warriors of Scandinavia. That is the mythology behind them. Historians have to go a little bit deeper than the fanciful tales to discover the truth behind these shock forces.

Berserkers traditionally prepared themselves for a fight. They permitted rage to take over, and their bodies would convulse with adrenaline rushes. Growling would indicate that they were ready for battle. However, this might not have been naturally induced.

One theory has it that they would get drunk before fighting. It could be the traditional mead drink or one that had some special herbs mixed into the beverage. Some scholars also believe a berserker was high on hallucinogenic mushrooms. Combining the ingredients of the mushroom with an already elevated state of anger would push the berserker into an uncontrollable rage. There are mushrooms in Scandinavia that do have hallucinogenic attributes.

Stories only embellish the image of these fighters. They reportedly went into battle wearing wolf pelts. They might also have gone into a conflict either naked or without armor. That could make this person dangerous because they had even greater freedom of movement.

One challenge with learning more about the berserker is there is so little physical evidence of them. Nevertheless, the rumor that berserkers were in the ranks of the Viking force would be sufficient to terrify any opponent.[34]

Viking Raiding Parties

Why were people so afraid of Ragnar and the other Vikings? The attack of a Viking longship could be dealt with. A levy of the local militia could easily overcome twenty or thirty people from a boat. There was something more to the raiding parties that struck terror into the hearts of people in England.

To begin with, being attacked by one dragon longship was not the standard method of operation. Professor Kenneth Harrell has estimated that a typical raiding party coming out of Scandinavia would have been as many as ten or twenty ships. When we do the math and calculate the number of vessels by a crew of fifty or sixty armed warriors, that raiding party grows to 500 to 1,200 battle-tested men.

The size of these raids grew over time. Viking incursions in the early 9th century might have seen up to one thousand warriors on twenty ships. That number would expand by the start of the 10th century to as many as one hundred ships and a force of five thousand to twelve thousand warriors. That is not just a simple raiding party; that is an invasion force!

It is estimated that the size of Viking raiding parties grew from three ships in the early 9th century to thirty or more ships by 850. This would mean that in the early days of the Viking Age, the raiding party would be no more than 150 warriors. The size of the strike force would be thirty ships or more by mid-century, and that means an invading force of 850 to 1500 men at arms. The later days of the ninth century might mean that a force of five thousand men would come in on hundreds of vessels.[35]

The English kingdoms were placed on the defensive because of Ragnar and other Vikings. The hit-and-run tactics of the Norsemen were difficult to counter because they were sudden and quick; Vikings were often gone before a relief force could appear on the scene.

---

[34] Warriors & Legends. (2023, August 20). *Viking Warrior Raids*. Retrieved from Warriorsandlegends.com: https://www.warriorsandlegends.com/viking-warriors/viking-warrior-raids/.

[35] Ulvog, J. (2017, November 8). *Size of Viking raiding parties*. Retrieved from Ancientfinances.com: https://ancientfinances.com/2017/11/08/size-of-viking-raiding-parties/#:~:text=In%20The%20Vikings%20course%20from,500%20up%20to%201%2C200%20warriors.

The situation in both England and Ireland is best described by a church antiphony of the time: "Our supreme and holy Grace, protecting us and ours, deliver us, God, from the savage race of Northmen which lays waste to our realms."[36]

Ragnar's death was suitably horrible. The *Gesta Danorum* records that King Ælla of Northumbria eventually captured him. We would think that a Viking like Ragnar would be hanged or beheaded, but there was a little theater in the way he was terminated. The king had his prisoner tossed into a pit of venomous snakes.

Ragnar reportedly took his death calmly and made an ominous comment before he perished: "How the little piglets would grunt if they knew how the old boar suffers."

Ragnar was referring to his sons and the revenge they would take on his killers when they learned what happened to him.

His sons would take revenge for the death of their father. These three warriors would sail to England with a substantial force of Danish Vikings. However, this was not going to be a large-scale raiding party. Instead, this was an invasion force that England had never seen before. The Danes did not come to burn down a monastery or pillage a village. Their intention was to stay, and the army led by Ragnar's sons was the most dangerous collection of men England had seen in hundreds of years.

---

[36] The Viking Answer Lady. (2023, August 29). *Origin of the phrase, "A furore Normannorum libera nos, Domine.* Retrieved from The Viking Answer Lady: http://www.vikinganswerlady.com/vikfury.shtml.

Chapter Three: The Great Heathen Army

The Anglo-Saxons should have known that there was something afoot. In 850, the Vikings were wintering in England. Additionally, large-scale Viking activities were happening. The *Anglo-Saxon Chronicle* mentions that 350 Viking ships sailed into the mouth of the Thames and attacked London. The Vikings put the Mercian king to flight and then went into Surrey. The Northmen were apparently not content to just raid along the coast. They were starting to go into the interior.

The Vikings were also being met by stiffer resistance than they had seen in the past. In 851, Æthelwulf fought a battle with the Vikings at Aclea and beat them. Another British victory occurred at Sandwich in 851 when King Æthelstan took on a Viking fleet and beat it. The conditions that had made Viking raids so successful in the past were starting to disappear. It was time for the Vikings to use a new tactic, one that would put them at greater risk but would also generate substantial rewards.

Viking raiders and traders were constantly bringing information back home to Scandinavia. There were still internal problems in Northumbria, and internal squabbling between the kingdoms was taking the focus away from dealing with larger threats. Moreover, the English kingdoms were becoming accustomed to paying off the Vikings. A tribute, which was a bribe more than anything else, seemed to be having a positive effect, making the Viking incursions a manageable threat.

A coordinated assault on England could produce substantial gains. It would require a major force to hit the British island and a military campaign that had tangible objectives. This sudden attack would throw the Anglo-Saxon kingdoms off balance and enable Viking raiders to penetrate deep into the countryside.

The idea of the Great Heathen Army probably originated in one of the drinking halls in Denmark. It would be a sustained effort to ravage England.

Origins of the Great Heathen Army

The story of this military force is complex, and there are conflicting stories. It appears that the desire to avenge Ragnar's death was the main reason for the formation of the army.

The Great Heathen Army was a coalition of Vikings from all over Scandinavia. The size of the army is estimated to have been between one thousand and three thousand men.

The force had a great banner under which they fought. It was called *hrafnsmerki*, and it depicted a raven flying upward.

Historians agree that the ultimate goal of this force was the domination of England. It is true that they were still looking for booty, but England was now more than just a raiding target. The Vikings were looking to take land in addition to treasure. England was looked at as a possible place to relocate families, settle down, and create a society with a Norse flavor to it. Each of the major kingdoms of the island would feel the fury of this force.[37]

The Viking Leaders

Ragnar Lothbrok had three sons who would become the leaders of the Great Heathen Army.

- Halfdan Ragnarsson

Halfdan is mentioned in Norse sagas as one of the six sons of Ragnar Lothbrok. He was a leader of the Great Heathen Army and is thought to have been the first Viking king of Northumbria. When the Great Heathen Army split, Halfdan led half of the army north into Northumbria and in attacks on Ireland. He also led his group against the Picts of Scotland and

---

[37] Kruljac, I. (2022, August 20). *The Great Heathen Army: What was it, and how did it unite the Vikings?* Retrieved from Thevikingherald.com: https://thevikingherald.com/article/the-great-heathen-army-what-was-it-and-how-did-it-unite-the-vikings/76.

the Scottish Kingdom of Strathclyde. Halfdan was reportedly killed at the Battle of Strangford Lough while trying to assert his claim to be king of Dublin.

The principal historical source for Halfdan is the *Annals of Ulster*. Coins minted in London in 872 and 873 have his name stamped on them and identify Halfdan as a leader of the Great Heathen Army.

- Ivar the Boneless

Ivar's name is rather unique. Some say it was a result of a curse. It might have been a genetic condition or possibly a mistranslation of an earlier text. We do not know the full story of why he was called the "Boneless." It might not have even been a physical condition at all. We know that Ivar was a very active Viking chief, and he was known for devastating raids. He was also a believer in brutal punishment, including the blood eagle, for anyone who crossed him.

Some stories claim that Ivar was a berserker who was driven by bloodlust. It is generally believed that he was very cunning and intelligent. He was also considered a very skilled tactician. While he was involved with the Great Heathen Army's invasion of England, Ivar is known for his later expeditions in Ireland.[38]

- Ubba

Scholars know the least about Ubba. He is mentioned in the *Passio sancti Eadmundi* as the man who killed King Edmund of East Anglia. He is also accused of having killed an abbess, Aebbe.[39]

Ragnar's sons were infuriated when they found out that their father had been killed. They attacked Northumbria and captured the Northumbrian king, Ælla. To avenge their father, they tortured their prisoner and used the blood eagle method to finish him off. (The blood eagle method required cutting open the victim's back and pulling their ribs and lungs out from behind.) Scholars are not certain this actually happened, but it makes for an amazing story and indicates how savage the Vikings could be when

---

[38] Sky History. (2023, August 20). *11 Facts About Fearsome Viking "Ivar the Boneless."* Retrieved from History.co.uk: https://www.history.co.uk/articles/11-facts-about-fearsome-viking-ivar-the-boneless.

[39] Williamson, J. (2022, August 20). *Who was Ubba Ragnarsson, the Viking commander of the Great Heathen Army?* Retrieved from Thevikingherald.com: https://thevikingherald.com/article/who-was-ubba-ragnarsson-the-viking-commander-of-the-great-heathen-army/194.

seeking revenge.[40]

The Initial Assault

The Great Heathen Army moved forward in 865. They already had a winter camp at Thanet, and they moved from there into East Anglia. The Anglo-Saxon Chronicle records the initial attack.

"This year sat the heathen army in the Isle of Thanet, and made peace with the men of Kent, who promised money therewith; but under the security of peace and the promise of money, the army in the night stole up the country and overran all Kent eastward."

There is an element of treachery in this. The Vikings were promised Danegeld, which was the customary way of solving the problem, but the raiders would not be satisfied with only that. Unbeknownst to the East Anglians, the Danes had bigger objectives in mind, and a few coffers of gold would not be sufficient.

King Edmund

History has been fairly kind to Edmund, King of East Anglia. He is portrayed as a pious man who was not moved by flattery. He would later be canonized and was one of the original patron saints of England.

It appears that King Edmund believed that tribute would get the Vikings out of his kingdom and allow them to go someplace else to do their mischief. It is reported that he gave the Great Heathen Army something they wanted more than gold: horses.

Given the objectives of the Vikings, it makes perfect sense that they would want horses more than gold coins. An army marching on foot takes time to get from one place to another. Marching through territory gives the occupants sufficient time to rally forces and strike back. Horses allow for speed. They can cover ground faster and enhance the element of surprise.

Edmund possibly thought that if he gave the Vikings the horses, they would trot off and bother somebody else. He no doubt figured that if he got them out of East Anglia, his troubles would be over. Time would show that Edmund made a horrible mistake and would pay for it dearly. The Vikings had the mounts they needed to move to the next objective.[41]

---

[40] Sky History. (2023, August 20). *11 Facts About Fearsome Viking "Ivar the Boneless."*

[41] Bishop, C. (2021, March 18). *Horses in battle at the time of Alfred the Great.* Retrieved from Historiamag.com: https://www.historiamag.com/horses-in-battle-at-the-time-of-alfred-the-great/#:~:text=King%20Edmund%20of%20East%20Anglia,of%20the%20horses%20they%20neede

Invasion of Northumbria

The Vikings knew the civil war in Northumbria had weakened the kingdom's ability to resist any incursion. Moreover, there was a score that needed to be settled with a certain king.

The Great Heathen Army wintered in Thetford and, in 866, made an ambitious advance across the Humber River into Northumbria. The destination was the city of York. This was a prosperous city and a prize worth taking. The *Anglo-Saxon Chronicle* records what the Danes did:

"The army went from the East-Angles over the mouth of the Humber to the Northumbrians, as far as York. There was an immense slaughter of the Northumbrians, some within and some without; and both the kings were slain on the spot. The survivors made peace with the army."

Despite the defenses of its Roman walls, York fell to Ivar the Boneless in 866, and the name of the city was changed to Jorvik.

Although it has been more than one thousand years since the Vikings were in the area, there are memories of the Northmen in the city. The best known is the suffix "gate," which is given to many streets in modern-day York. It comes from the Viking word *gata*, meaning "street."[42]

The Northumbrians rallied and made an attempt to retake York. Unfortunately, they failed miserably. On March 23rd, 867, Earl Osberht, a claimant to the throne, was killed, and King Ælla was captured and supposedly tortured to death. The two principal leaders of Northumbria had been killed. The Vikings installed a new king, Ecgberht, as a sovereign. He was a puppet, and his only function was to hold down the fort and collect taxes for the Vikings, who were now looking for another prize to plunder.

---

d.
[42] Britain Express. (2023, August 20). *Viking York*. Retrieved from Britainexpress.com: https://www.britainexpress.com/cities/york/viking.htm.

Mercia's Turn

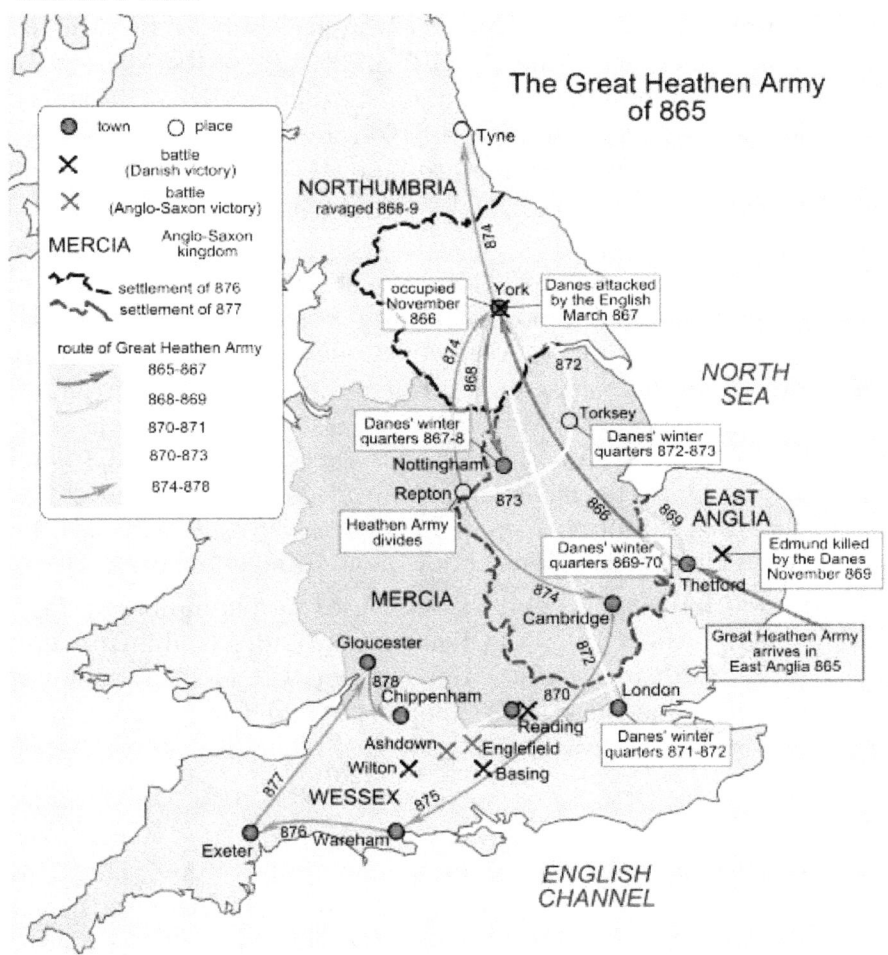

The routes the Great Heathen Army took.
Hel-hama, CC BY-SA 3.0 <https://creativecommons.org/licenses/by-sa/3.0>, via Wikimedia Commons; https://commons.wikimedia.org/wiki/File:England_Great_Army_map.svg

A map of the Great Heathen Army's progress shows that the Vikings crossed Mercia to get to York. It appears strange that the Mercians did not mount a fierce resistance at that time, but they might have been under the misapprehension that all the Vikings were going to do was raid Northumbria and go home. Once again, an Anglo-Saxon kingdom made a terrible mistake. The *Anglo-Saxon Chronicle* continued its story of what the Great Heathen Army was doing. The tale starts with the winter quartering in 867/68.

"This year the same army went into Mercia to Nottingham, and there fixed their winter quarters; and Burhred [Burgred], king of the Mercians, with his counsel, besought Ethered [Æthelred], king of the West-Saxons, and Alfred, his brother; that they would assist them in fighting against the army. And they went with the West-Saxon army into Mercia as far as Nottingham and there meeting the army on the works, they beset them within. But there was no heavy fight; for the Mercians made peace with the army."

To provide some context to the *Anglo-Saxon Chronicle*, the Great Heathen Army established winter quarters at Nottingham, and Mercia was in a quandary. This was the moment when one of the British kings came to his senses about the Viking threat. Burgred, the king of Mercia, knew he had to get help in order to drive the invaders out. He sought assistance from Æthelred. The *Anglo-Saxon Chronicle* refers to him as the king of the West Saxons, which means they came from Wessex, the Anglo-Saxon kingdom that took up most of southern England. Wessex agreed to help Mercia, and an allied force marched north to retake Nottingham.

The city was under siege, and the Vikings were outnumbered. It is at this point that the Anglo-Saxons' inability to fully understand their enemy's goals handicapped their resistance. Burgred negotiated a peace treaty with the Vikings. The Danes were allowed to keep Nottingham in exchange for leaving the rest of Mercia alone. It was a blunder that had terrible consequences later on.[43]

Back to East Anglia

The Great Heathen Army was not just one military unit. There were several forces, each under the command of one of Ragnar's sons. Peace was established in Mercia, and the Vikings looked for someplace else to attack. They fixed their eyes on East Anglia.

This was when it became clear that Edmund had made a terrible misjudgment a few years earlier. He was able to secure peace for his kingdom but only for a brief amount of time. A more prudent sovereign would have recognized that the alliance between Mercia and Wessex meant that the Vikings were more than just a bunch of raiders and pirates.

Unfortunately, Edmund underestimated his enemy, and the *Anglo-Saxon Chronicle* tells the story of what happened in East Anglia in 869:

---

[43] English Monarchs. (2023, August 20). *The Danelaw*. Retrieved from Englishmonarchs.com: https://www.englishmonarchs.co.uk/vikings_11.html

"This year the army rode over Mercia into East-Anglia, and there fixed their winter-quarters at Thetford. And in the winter King Edmund fought with them; but the Danes gained the victory, and slew the king; whereupon they overran all that land, and destroyed all the monasteries to which they came. The names of the leaders who slew the king were Hingwar and Hubba."[44]

Edmund died a vicious death, but we need to be objective about the facts in this matter. East Anglia was defeated in battle, and Edmund was captured. Ivar the Boneless offered to allow Edmund to live if he would renounce his Christian faith. The devout Christian that he was, Edmund refused. The Viking leader then ordered Edmund to be tied to a tree. The East Anglian king was first beaten with cudgels and then whipped. It is believed that Edmund continued to call upon the name of Jesus Christ throughout all of this torture. Ivar was exasperated by the show of piety, and he allowed his troops to use Edmund for target practice. The story has it that Edmund's body looked like that of a porcupine after the target practice was finished. His head was then cut off.[45]

Edmund became Saint Edmund, and a cult of devotion to the martyr developed. He represented a fierce Christian resistance to the heathen Vikings, and he was venerated up until the 16th century. Nevertheless, we have to look at this man with critical eyes. Edmund gave the Vikings the horses they needed to rapidly advance into the middle of England. It appears that he was more concerned with getting the marauders out of East Anglia and did not realize what the long-term consequences of his decision would be. He paid a terrible price for his mistake, but he was not the only monarch who made a bad decision when dealing with the Vikings. Ultimately, only one of the kings of England had a fair assessment of the danger, and he was the one who would vanquish the Great Heathen Army.

The Vikings met with success after success in five years. Northumbria became a puppet state, Mercia paid Danegeld to keep the peace, and East Anglia was devastated. Norse immigrants were beginning to settle in the areas that the Great Heathen Army subjugated.

---

[44] Medieval Archives. (2020, November 20). *King Edmund the Martyr Killed by the Great Heathen Army*. Retrieved from Medievalarchives.com: https://medievalarchives.com/2020/11/20/king-edmund-the-martyr-killed-by-the-great-heathen-army/.

[45] New Advent. (2023, August 20). *St. Edmund the Martyr*. Retrieved from Newadvent.org: https://www.newadvent.org/cathen/05295a.htm.

Ivar the Boneless took time off from the English raids. He partnered up with Olaf the White, a Norse king in Ireland, and together, they raided Scotland and sacked Dumbarton.[46]

Looking South to Wessex

There was only one kingdom left for the Vikings to subjugate, and that was Wessex. The morale of the Great Heathen Army was no doubt very high, but it might have gained too much overconfidence.

Wessex was one of the seven major Anglo-Sason kingdoms of the Heptarchy (East Anglia, Mercia, Northumbria, Wessex, Sussex, Essex, and Kent). Wessex would eventually absorb Sussex and be the primary power in southern and southwestern England.

It would prove to be a tough nut to crack, and its rulers were not the type of people who gave up easily. The campaigns in the south would be very different.

Wessex was blessed with advantages its neighbors lacked. It had a strong economy that was centered on agriculture, with some tin mining thrown into the mix. Unlike Northumbria at the time, Wessex was not racked by internal civil war or aristocratic bickering. Unlike East Anglia, it was not ruled by an overly pious person who could not see potential danger. Wessex economy and a stable ruling class gave southern England a better chance of dealing with the Great Heathen Army.

The king of Wessex at the time was Æthelred. He was the son of Æthelwulf and became king in 865 when he was only around twenty years old after his older brother, Æthelberht, had died. The new king was faced with having to deal with the Great Heathen Army and the severe threat to his kingdom.

Æthelred was not intimidated by the Vikings, and he was not about to pay the invaders a bribe. He allied with the Mercians and helped his neighbor try to retake Nottingham. That effort failed, and the Mercians were forced to sue for peace. However, Æthelred was undeterred. He was prepared to continue resisting the Great Heathen Army despite having to do it alone.

---

[46] Lewis, R. (2023, August 20). *Ivar the Boneless*. Retrieved from Brittanica.com: https://www.britannica.com/biography/Ivar-the-Boneless.

The Invasion of Wessex

The Vikings decided that Wessex would be their next victim, and they launched an assault on that kingdom at the end of 870. Æthelred and his brother Alfred were defeated at Reading, but a few days later, they won a victory at the Battle of Ashdown. The West Saxons lost at Basing and Meretun, but Æthelred still had an army in the field. He was going to need it shortly.

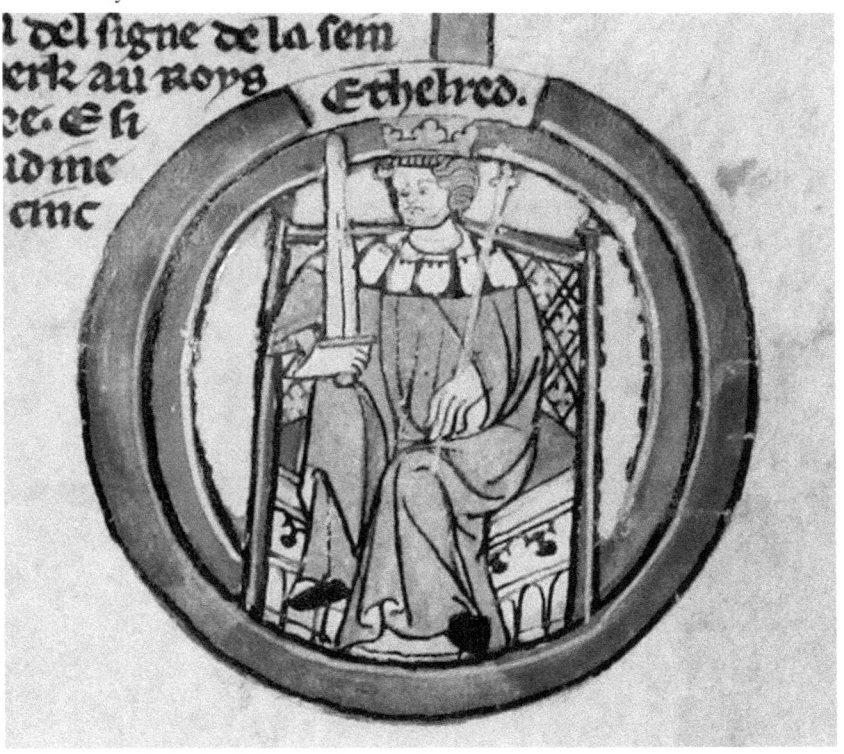

An illustration of Æthelred.
https://commons.wikimedia.org/wiki/File:%C3%86thelred_-_MS_Royal_14_B_VI.jpg

The Vikings received reinforcements from the Great Summer Army, which was commanded by Guthrum, who was a nephew of the Danish king. These troops arrived in April 871 and joined the rest of the Vikings at Reading. Æthelred died shortly after Easter in 871 and was succeeded by his younger brother Alfred. The story of Alfred and the Great Heathen Army will be discussed in greater detail in the following chapters. Suffice it to say for now, Alfred was up against an enormous obstacle.

The Great Heathen Army totally disrupted any sense of order in England. Three of the four kingdoms were devastated, and the damage done to the economy was substantial. The best lesson to be drawn from the experience was the penalty to be paid for lacking a united front.

Northumbria, Mercia, East Anglia, and Wessex might have stopped the Viking incursion in its early stages had they been united in an alliance against the seafaring foe. They were not, and as one kingdom collapsed, the others were desperately trying to find a way to placate the Danes. Only Wessex appreciated the risk of having a foreign army deep in the heart of England. As a result, they faced the Great Heathen Army, knowing that the existence of their kingdom was on the line. No bribe or tribute was going to stop the enemy from obtaining its ultimate goal of complete conquest.

The history of England was turning to a darker page. There seemed to be nothing that could stop the Great Heathen Army. It was at this time in English history that a man stepped forward to confront the foe. All accounts admit he was a great man.

Chapter Four: Alfred the Great

To date, Alfred was the only English monarch to have "the Great" placed after his name. When anyone looks at what Alfred accomplished during his life, that person can immediately recognize why that is so. Alfred justifiably earned that honor, and his reputation is based on facts, not legends.

English history has instances where a person of courage and audacity, such as Elizabeth I or Winston Churchill, stepped forward to lead the nation in a time of crisis. Alfred was one of those who prevented England from spiraling into an abyss. He became the king of Wessex when an epoch in English history might have ended in a cataclysmic disaster.

Alfred was the son of Æthelwulf and his wife, Osburh. The old king had five sons, and four of them would go on to rule over Wessex. The Wessex line of succession shows a peaceful transfer from one brother to another since most of the brothers did not have heirs. There is also evidence that a brother would help his ruling sibling in times of danger. This might be one of the reasons why the Kingdom of Wessex had a stable monarchy and a society that was not prone to civil war.

Accession to Power

Alfred provided assistance to his brother during the fierce resistance against the incursions of the Great Heathen Army into Wessex. However, Æthelred died, leaving behind infant sons. The kingdom was in a severe predicament and could not afford to have a child on the throne. Alfred had an understanding of the dangers Wessex faced, having been on the front lines of the resistance from the beginning of the Great Heathen

Army's invasion in 865. The country's ruling class decided to bypass the small children and give Alfred the crown.

The Vikings now controlled the eastern half of England. Having beaten or cowed the other three Anglo-Saxon kingdoms, the foreign army was now able to turn all of its resources and might against the southern kingdom.

Alfred continued the fight, but he was facing an adversary that was relentless. He was faced with no other alternative but to find a way to buy peace. Fortunately for him, the Viking commanders, Guthrum and Halfdan, were willing to listen to his terms.

It is not that surprising that the Vikings were amenable to negotiation. They had been fighting for over six years and had suffered losses. Their casualties were high, and morale was starting to sink. The opportunities for plunder were vanishing, and there was a growing desire in the ranks to settle their families in the newly conquered lands. Nevertheless, the price for peace was going to be stiff.

Alfred was required to pay an annual payment of Danegeld and cede eastern England to the Vikings. This meant that, by 873, the Vikings had control of East Anglia, Northumbria, Mercia, and the eastern section of Wessex. Alfred was willing to concede to the conditions. The Wessex king realized he had to buy time to make a stand.[47]

Viking Worries

The Great Heathen Army had wintered in late 871, no doubt welcoming the rest from the ongoing fighting. Their leaders needed to reassess their priorities and determine their next moves. Halfdan noticed some problems were occurring in the north. The Northumbrians had been defeated, but that did not mean they were satisfied with their new overlords. There was a rebellion against Ecgberht that needed to be suppressed. The Mercians paid the Danegeld to keep the peace, but there were problems underneath the surface. In 873, Ivar the Boneless died. Halfdan lost a valuable war chief.

Burgred was going to learn that paying off the Vikings didn't guarantee security for his throne. The Great Heathen Army attacked Mercia in 874, and Burgard was forced to flee for his life. He eventually went into exile in

---

[47] MacNeil, R. (2019, May). *The Great Heathen Failure: Why the Great Heathen Army Failed to Conquer the Whole of Anglo-Saxon England.* Retrieved from Digitalcommons.winthrop.edu: https://digitalcommons.winthrop.edu/cgi/viewcontent.cgi?article=1105&context=graduatetheses.

Rome and died there. The Vikings now had complete control over Mercia.[48]

It was apparent to the Viking commanders that there was nothing more to accomplish as a united force. In addition, Northumbria and Mercia needed to be watched, and any possible rebellions had to be put down. It was a time when permanent residence in England was the new Viking priority.

In 874, the Great Heathen Army divided. Halfdan went north and began the process of settling his men in the lands they had conquered. Guthrum remained behind with his portion of the army. Although Alfred would facie Guthrum in the coming years, he would be confronting a much smaller enemy force.[49]

The Wessex Campaign

Peace did not mean that Alfred was enjoying the quiet. He used this time to reestablish his authority in Wessex and recruit an army. Unlike his fellow Anglo-Saxon kings, Alfred did not trust the Vikings to honor the peace or remain inactive. He kept an army ready for any new outbreak of war. It was a very smart strategy.

Guthrum attacked in 875. He was using a course of action that succeeded in the past: occupying a town and waiting for a chance to receive money in return for a promise to leave. They did this in Wareham. Alfred was not able to take Wareham and negotiated a peace treaty with Guthrum. The Vikings promptly broke their word and killed the hostages that Alfred had provided. They moved into Exeter, where Alfred successfully blockaded the Viking ships. The Vikings negotiated a peace with Alfred in late 877 and retreated to Gloucester. However, they still kept their goal of gaining control over all of Wessex.

Alfred wintered in Chippenham for Christmas in 877. The Danes attacked Alfred in January 878 and forced Alfred to flee with a small group of men into the wilderness. The Vikings had the upper hand, but they did not have the king.

---

[48] Discovery. (2023, May 3). *Who was King Burgred of Mercia and what did he do?* Retrieved from Discoveryuk.com: https://www.discoveryuk.com/monarchs-and-rulers/who-was-king-burgred-of-mercia-and-what-did-he-do/.

[49] MacNeil, R. (2019, May). *The Great Heathen Failure: Why the Great Heathen Army Failed to Conquer the Whole of Anglo-Saxon England.*

Some historians criticize Alfred, saying that he was not able to defeat the Danes in open-field combat successfully. He seemed more prone to pay off the Vikings and get them to leave for a while.

After the near disaster at Chippenham, Alfred was a monarch with a barely effective fighting force. Fortunately for Wessex, events were about to change. The year 878 proved to be a very decisive one.

The Burning Cakes

Alfred escaped after nearly being taken prisoner and fled into hiding. He found refuge in the marshes of Somerset and laid low on the Isle of Athelney. Here is where one of the more delightful legends about King Alfred originated.

Alfred was in a small hut. He was asked by the lady of the house to watch over some griddle cakes (small bread loaves). Alfred agreed, but he was so distracted by his worries over what to do that he completely forgot his chore. The cakes burned, and the woman was furious. Legend has it that she scolded and even beat the king of Wessex with a broom. Alfred did not tell her that he was the king and graciously accepted his punishment. The story shows King Alfred to be not just a regal person but also somebody who was fair. He did something wrong, apologized for it, and did not try to punish the lady for her behavior.

There is no way we can check this story's accuracy because there is no record of it from the time. Actually, it was not mentioned at all until several hundred years after it supposedly took place. Nevertheless, it depicts a man who was willing to accept punishment, and it enhances the legend of Alfred the Great.[50]

The Battle of Edington

Alfred knew he had to strike back and hit the invaders as hard as possible. He waited until the spring of 878 and then sent out a call to his army to assemble at a place known as Egbert's Stone. Once the troops had assembled, Alfred marched them to Edington. There, at some point between May 6th and May 12th, 878, Alfred and his army fought an engagement with the Danes. Alfred's soldiers formed a shield wall and were able to provide stiff resistance. This time, the Danes were beaten. The *Anglo-Saxon Chronicle* gives an account of what happened next.

---

[50] Pearce, S. (2023, February 16). *Where King Alfred Burnt Cakes in Athelney-King Alfred's Monument!* Retrieved from Third Eye Traveler: https://thirdeyetraveller.com/where-king-alfred-burnt-cakes-in-athelney-king-alfreds-monument/.

"He [Alfred] pursued them as far as their fortress [Chippenham] and besieged them therefore fortnight. This time it was the Vikings who had to give in and sue for peace. They gave him hostages and swore great oaths to leave the kingdom, and also that their king would receive baptism."[51]

The Treaty of Wedmore

After the Battle of Edington, Alfred and Guthrum entered into an agreement over the new status quo in England. It defined the boundary between Wessex and the Viking holdings, recognizing all of what is now south and southwestern England as belonging to King Alfred and Wessex.

The significance of this agreement cannot be understated. The Danes realized there was a limit to their territory. The treaty also required Guthrum to agree to be baptized as a Christian.

Guthrum provided hostages who could be immediately killed if he broke the treaty. Historians have noted that this treaty was the beginning of the historical process that ultimately led to a unified Kingdom of England. Alfred won an immense victory through persistence and courage.

However, this did not mean that the problems with the Vikings went away. There were still raids and incursions into Wessex.

Alfred had successfully fought back the Danes, using both his army and fleet. However, he realized there had to be a permanent form of defense against the Danes to ultimately discourage them from ever trying to successfully raid his territory.

The Burgh System

Alfred developed a defensive policy that centered on creating fortified towns known as burghs. The basic plan was simple. People were encouraged to settle within these towns in exchange for free plots of land. This created a system of fortified places no more than twenty miles from a town. A Viking raiding party would be within a day's march of a local militia. The burghs also gave farmers a place to find protection.

Alfred enhanced the defensive posture of the burghs by building roads that interconnected them. The Vikings were now in a situation where they might be cut off from any escape if they attacked a place. The Northmen did not like the idea of having too many casualties for no reward, so they

---

[51] Anglo-Saxon.net. (2023, August 21). *Early-Medieval-England.net Timeline: 871-899.* Retrieved from Anglo-Saxon.net: http://www.anglo-saxons.net/hwact/?do=seek&query=871-899.

had to think twice before they ventured into Wessex.

The roads that connected the burghs were also used for trade and other commerce. Alfred essentially created economic centers within his kingdom that could be used to improve the overall economy.

This plan was extensive. As listed in the Burghal Hidage, an Anglo-Saxon document, more than thirty burghs were created.[52]

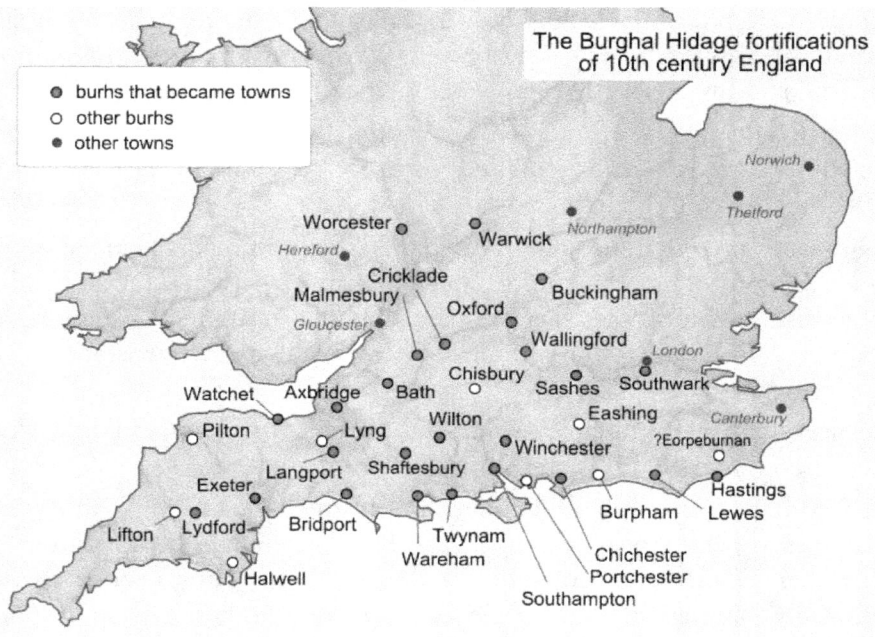

Map of the burghs listed in the Burghal Hidage.
Hel-hama, CC BY-SA 3.0 <https://creativecommons.org/licenses/by-sa/3.0>, via Wikimedia Commons; https://commons.wikimedia.org/wiki/File:Anglo-Saxon_burhs.svg

Further Defenses

The Vikings continued to raid the territory held by King Alfred. A major seaborne attack occurred in 893 that was different than some of the earlier raids. The Vikings brought their families with them with the intention of colonizing. Alfred was able to meet these attacks and outmaneuver his enemies.

---

[52] The History Junkie. (2023, August 21). *5 Reasons That Burhs Were Important and How They Helped Alfred the Great Defeat the Vikings.* Retrieved from Thehistoryjunkie.com: https://thehistoryjunkie.com/5-reasons-that-burhs-were-important-and-how-they-helped-alfred-the-great-defeat-the-vikings/.

One of the changes Alfred made involved sea defense. In 896, he ordered the construction of a small fleet of longships that were each twice the size of a Viking raiding vessel. Although it was not the birth of the English navy, it increased the naval power of Wessex.

Alfred had ships that were swifter, larger, steadier, and rode higher in the water than the Viking boats. He was able to intercept the raiding parties as they were coming across the water, making his kingdom that much safer.

Alfred and Education

Alfred was more than a warrior. He was an innovator and a reformer who brought about significant changes in his kingdom. When he visited Rome, he stayed with Frankish King Charles the Bald and discussed with him how the Carolingian kings were able to deal with the Vikings.

Alfred knew that he needed money to pay for his defenses, so he expanded taxation and based what a person owed on the productivity of that individual's land holdings. A hide was the basic unit for assessing tax obligations. It was the amount of land required to support one's family and would differ in size. Landowners were required to provide services or money based on how many hides that individual owned.

Alfred wanted to create an educational system that would rival the one created by Charlemagne. Court schools were established to educate the nobility and those who were of lower social rank. The curriculum was dedicated to the liberal arts.[53]

Alfred was different from someone who wanted to learn for the sake of learning. He was concerned about the proper execution of justice and sought a better understanding of how to live according to divine principles.

Alfred declared himself king of the Anglo-Saxons in 886. He left behind a kingdom that was in a better situation than when he had found it upon his coronation. His educational reforms, his success in military ventures, and his attempts to preserve the peace and stability of Wessex are all reasons why he is referred to as "Great." We have to admit that his reign was a remarkable period of time in which the character of Anglo-Saxon England was changed for the better.

---

[53] European Royal History. (2022, October 22). *October 26, 899: Death of Alfred the Great, King of the Anglo-Saxons.* Retrieved from Europeanroyalhistory.com:
https://europeanroyalhistory.wordpress.com//?s=Alfred+the+Great&search=Go.

It no longer made sense for the Vikings to plunder and destroy the countryside. There was much more to be gained by tilling the fields and engaging in commerce.

Peace was no longer just a pastime to indulge in when the weather was terrible. The Vikings and their families were settling into an area of what is now modern England. It was known as the Danelaw. It lasted for less than one hundred years but left an indelible mark on the English countryside. It is well worth exploring the changes it delivered.

Chapter Five: The Danelaw

The invasion of the Great Heathen Army in 865 was the high watermark of the Viking incursions into England. In the years that followed, the intensity of the Viking attacks began to lessen. There are some primary reasons for the decrease in sea-raiding violence.

Anglo-Saxon communities developed strategies to deal with the marauders. The burgh system established by Alfred the Great created a network of fortified towns that could resist the Vikings, and the local militias were better organized. Alfred's navy could now meet the incoming sea rovers on the open waters. That was a far cry from waiting on the beaches, searching for a dragon longship appearing on the horizon. The Vikings were brave men, but they were not reckless. Attacking a fortified place that was expecting them and ready to inflict severe casualties was too much of a risk.

Guthrum converted to Christianity, and he was not the only Northman to do so. Others accepted the way of the cross, perhaps not always because of a come-to-Jesus moment. Being a Christian offered some possibilities for commercial enterprise, and trade provided more reliable profits than raids. Peaceful activities, such as farming, were tempting alternatives to the slash-and-burn existence of earlier days.

Besides, the Vikings succeeded in their objective of obtaining land in England. Northumbria, Mercia, and East Anglia were under the control of Viking overlords, and the Treaty of Wedmore established fixed boundaries between Wessex and Viking-held land. A new political entity, the Danelaw, came into being.

Creation of a Land of Danes

It was known as *Danelagen* in Danish and *Dena lagu* in Old English. The Danelaw was a recognition that the Vikings were in England to stay. Modern students of history sometimes forget that the Vikings were not just pirates. They were also farmers and exceptional blacksmiths. They had established communities in Scandinavia, and they brought their societies to Anglo-Saxon England. The territory the Vikings inhabited spread from London to East Anglia and through the Midlands up to the north of England.[54]

The significant founding document of the Danelaw was the Treaty of Wedmore. Guthrum had no desire to break the treaty that he had signed, and he was ready to retire from being a marauding nuisance. Danish Mercia was under the control of five Danish armies, which introduced their native laws and customs to this middle section of England. There were five main towns or boroughs established in this Viking-held area: Derby, Leicester, Lincoln, Nottingham, and Stamford. These were all fortified municipalities.

Fifteen shires of modern England would become the Danelaw. These included Leicester, Nottingham, Derby, Lincoln, York, Essex, Cambridge, Suffolk, Northampton, Norfolk, Huntington, Bedford, Middlesex Hertford, and Buckinghamshire.

Important Danelaw Centers

Nottingham was one of the principal towns. The Danish settlement officially started in 877. Derby was settled in 877. The borough of Lincoln was a strategic holding; it was on the route between Wessex and York. Leicester would be the scene of several military engagements while it was part of the Danelaw.[55]

---

[54] Roua, V. (2016, May 7). *A Brief History of the Danish Vikings and of the Danelaw.* Retrieved from Thedockyards.com: https://www.thedockyards.com/the-danish-vikings-and-the-danelaw/.
[55] Brain, J. (2023, August 26). *The Five Boroughs of Danelaw.* Retrieved from Historic-uk.com: https://www.historic-uk.com/HistoryUK/HistoryofEngland/The-Five-Boroughs-Of-Danelaw/.

The Danelaw in 878.
Hel-hama, CC BY-SA 3.0 <https://creativecommons.org/licenses/by-sa/3.0>, via Wikimedia Commons; https://commons.wikimedia.org/wiki/File:England_878.svg)

The Population

We do not know precisely how many Scandinavians decided to settle in the Danelaw. While it was an opportunity to expand in a new region, not everybody was willing to leave their old homes for a new place. Only a few thousand might have migrated.

These immigrants intermingled with the Anglo-Saxons. Because of this, a language was created that was a combination of Old Norse and Old English. Both dialects had a Germanic origin and were similar in many ways. A difference between the two was in the rules of grammar, which could cause some confusion until the two were blended into one.

An Anglo-Norse dialect ultimately developed, and traditional dialects in Yorkshire, Lancashire, the Lake District, and Lincolnshire can trace their roots to this patois.[56]

Commerce and Trade in the Danelaw

The towns of the Danelaw became part of the Scandinavian trading network. This was a commercial highway that dominated northern Europe for centuries and fostered the commercial development of an expanse that covered all of Scandinavia, Britain, Ireland, and as far west as Iceland. The trading towns included places far away as Kyiv, Novgorod, Rouen, Wolin, Dublin, and Truso.[57] The common goods that were traded included slaves, furs, textiles, and iron goods. Imports, such as spices from Byzantium, would enrich the societies that were part of the trade network. Products that had not been seen in Anglo-Saxon England before were being introduced thanks to the extensive trade network.[58]

There were centers of significant trade activity in the Danelaw. York, known as Jorvik to the Danes, was the best example. Excavations in the York area suggest the diversity of goods that entered Anglo-Saxon England because of the Danelaw's trading network.

Manufacturing activities in the Danelaw included glass, leather, and metalwork. Jewelry and dress accessories from Scotland and Ireland were found, along with cowry shells from the Mediterranean and walrus ivory that was imported from Norway.

Scandinavian ships could sail up the Humber and then navigate the Ouse River to York, thanks to the shallow draft of the boats. Trade goods could be taken overland to the west coast and loaded on ships headed for Dublin, Ireland. Other Irish ports included Cork, Waterford, Wexford, and Limerick, which were all trading destinations for Danelaw merchants.

Land travel was possible from York through trails in the valleys. York is situated on a broad, flat plain that stretches south to north and goes through northern England. This meant merchant trade caravans could go

---

[56] Viking.no. (2004, August 14). *The Danelaw: Population, culture and heritage.* Retrieved from Viking.no: https://www.viking.no/e/england/danelaw/e-heritage-danelaw.htm.

[57] Skjaden. (2020, January 16). *Trade in the Viking Age-Do You Know Which Trade Towns That Were the Most Important Ones?* Retrieved from Nordic Culture: https://skjalden.com/where-did-the-vikings-trade/.

[58] Skald, F. t. (2016, September 16). *Viking History: Post-by-Post.* Retrieved from Fjorn-the-skald.tumblr.com: https://fjorn-the-skald.tumblr.com/post/150515624715/lesson-16-viking-money-commerce-coins-and.

north to Scotland or south to Nottingham and Derby.[59]

Law and Administration

The idea of trial by combat and blood feuds makes for exciting television shows, but that is not how affairs were managed in the Danelaw. There was a system of legal practice and administration that permitted society to function in an orderly fashion. The Danelaw's legal system was based on Scandinavian law.

However, the Danelaw's legal practices differed from Anglo-Saxon England. The penalty for killing a person in the Danelaw was determined by a person's social status. Punishments for crimes related to royal jurisdiction in Anglo-Saxon England were significantly harsher, and the spheres of offenses were broader.

The area of the Five Boroughs (Derby, Leicester, Lincoln, Nottingham, and Stamford) had an extensive organization of the judicial system, which included county courts and village court meetings. This system gave rise to the use of juries in English common law. Juries were a feature of Scandinavian jurisprudence, which had previously been unknown in the Anglo-Saxon regions.

The free peasantry, as opposed to serfdom, was a feature of the Danelaw. The idea of a manorial system that relied on feudal ties between a lord and his serfs was not common in the Danelaw. Free farmers were descendants of soldiers and colonists. There was a special category, the sokemen, who were obliged to perform minor duties for their lord, such as paying small rent payments and helping in the fields during harvest. However, these people had complete ownership of their land plots. The relationship with their lord was contractual, not inherited. While the Norman invasion in the 11th century would change things, the sokemen could still be found in East Anglia and the area of the Five Boroughs for centuries.

The social freedom in the Danelaw led the area to become one of the most prosperous regions of England. Free men turned the forests and wastelands into arable farmland and improved the region's agricultural activity. The innovations and customs that Viking immigrants introduced would serve as models for future English society.[60]

---

[59] Viking.no. (2004, August 14). *Trade routes in the British Isles.* Retrieved from Viking.no: https://www.viking.no/e/england/york/jorvik_trading_centre_2.html.
[60] Chakra, H. (2021, September 27). *The Story of Danelaw.* Retrieved from About-history.com:

Coinage

A fascinating aspect of the Danelaw's commercial practices was the use of coins. It may seem to be a minor item, but coins permit an economy to make the exchange of goods more manageable. The reason is simple. The alternative would be to use another product or metal bullion to pay for something. It would require either the appraisal of the other trade goods or weight measures to determine how much bullion to pay.

Norsemen originally used a bullion economy and weighed the metal for commercial transactions. The new settlers in the Danelaw were familiar with coins because Danegeld was paid in Anglo-Saxon currency.

Interaction with other foreign trading zones showed the importance of using coins, and in the mid-890s, national coinage was introduced within the Danelaw. Coinage has been found in excavations in York and sites in East Anglia, although not in plentiful numbers. Christian imagery, such as the Christian cross, was commonly found on Danelaw coinage. Bullion was still used, particularly in rural areas, but mints were established in places like York.

Examples of Viking coins.
The Portable Antiquities Scheme/ The Trustees of the British Museum, CC BY-SA 4.0 <https://creativecommons.org/licenses/by-sa/4.0>, via Wikimedia Commons; https://commons.wikimedia.org/wiki/File:Thurcaston_Viking_mixed_coin_hoard_(FindID_106146).jpg

https://about-history.com/the-story-of-danelaw/.

Interaction with the Anglo-Saxons

The former sea raiders became more established in England in the 10th century and were involved in diplomacy in the Anglo-Saxon Kingdom of Wessex. Language barriers existed, and they had to be overcome in order to have stable and peaceful relations. As mentioned, Norse words gradually found their way into the developing English language.

Linguistic experts speak of the concept of loanwords. These were infused into English by Old Norse, and it is estimated that around six hundred loaned words are part of today's standard English.

Some of the English words we use every day were derived from Scandinavian sources. Anger, berserk, ransack, and slaughter reflect the age of the Viking raids. Not all of the expressions were violent, though. Sky, skip, happy, and glitter all have origins in Old Norse or Scandinavian languages.

Days of the week, such as Thursday, came from the Vikings. And some useful words like get, take, and they came from the Northmen.[61]

The Domesday Book, a survey of England completed by William the Conqueror, provides evidence that Scandinavian loanwords were becoming more familiar and were being frequently used. Forty percent of the East Riding of Yorkshire's place names recorded in the Domesday Book have Scandinavian origins. Additionally, 50 percent of the names from Nottingham and Cheshire were Scandinavian. It is argued that this reflects naming conventions, not that there were a large number of Scandinavians in those areas.[62]

Christianity and the Danelaw

Guthrum's conversion was the first significant religious change to affect the new settlers in Anglo-Saxon England. The trend toward Christianity would increase in the 10th century as trade between the Norse and the Anglo-Saxons began to grow. Christianity became a common bond between the Anglo-Saxons and the Danes. Becoming Christian made sense to Norse traders because interactions were much more manageable. It also made Norse settlers more accepted in Anglo-Saxon and European

---

[61] Sky History. (2023, August 26). *Old Norse Words We Use Every Day.* Retrieved from www.history.co.uk: https://www.history.co.uk/shows/vikings/articles/old-norse-words-we-use-every-day.

[62] Fi, B. a. (2015, May 2). *Vikings in the Danelaw.* Retrieved from Babiafi.co.uk: https://www.babiafi.co.uk/2015/05/vikings-in-danelaw.html.

society.

Christianity allowed for a degree of pacification of people who were accustomed to violence. Values such as charity and community service were embraced, and these values, among others, helped in the "domestication" of the sea raiders. There would still be some traces of the Vikings' old customs in folklore and festivals, but Christianity eventually became a fixture in the Danelaw.

The raiders who once burned and pillaged monasteries helped build new ones, and the Archbishopric of York gradually became a vital Christian center in England. An example of Christianity triumphing over the old Norse practices is Oswald of Worcester. He was the archbishop of York from 972 to 992, and he was committed to church reform. Oswald had Danish ancestry and later became a saint.

Christianity was also a means of ensuring domestic peace within the Danelaw. Not every inhabitant of the Danelaw was from Scandinavia. Toleration of Christianity made it easier for the Norse overlords to administer their territories and keep the Anglo-Saxon population loyal to them.

Interestingly, cemeteries in Britain give examples of religious integration. There is evidence of pagan burials, and Christian crosses engraved with Scandinavian art have been found on the Isle of Man. The new settlers were willing to incorporate artistic designs with standard Christian imagery.

Guthrum eventually retired to East Anglia and reigned over the Kingdom of Guthrum until his death.

Peaceful relations between the Danes and the Anglo-Saxons did not always last for very long. Friction between the two sides became worse.

The primary difference between the opening years of the 10th century and what had happened before was that the shoe was now on the other foot. The successor of Alfred the Great, Edward the Elder, did not want a potential enemy on his northern border. Aggressive campaigns were fought against the Danes in the Danelaw and in Danish Northumbria. A treaty was signed in 906, but it did not last because Edward harassed the Northumbrian Danes in 909. Edward continued his offensives against the Danes and, by 912, had gained control of the southern Danelaw. The following years saw Edward defeating the Danes in several battles.

Edward the Elder was part of the resurgence of Anglo-Saxon England. The Anglo-Saxons were not as fractious as they had been in earlier years;

rather, they were uniting under the king of the Anglo-Saxons.

The downfall of the Danelaw was also caused by internal struggles that drew attention away from the military threat creeping up from the south.

Cultural assimilation weakened the ties with the Norse culture. Intermarriage caused the Scandinavians to lose their distinctive identity as they mingled more and more frequently with Anglo-Saxons. The use of Old English became more frequent, and Christianity strengthened the connections with the Anglo-Saxons.

The Scandinavians were no longer a unique group, and they were facing an enemy that presented a united front against them. It was the Anglo-Saxons who now desired to have control over the country. The rulers of the Danelaw were increasingly at a disadvantage.

Æthelstan, the son of Edward the Elder, continued the aggressive policy against the Danelaw. The former Vikings were gradually being forced back from their original holdings. Anglo-Saxons benefited from a more organized military strategy and political alliances. The Danelaw ceased to be a political entity in 954 when Eric Bloodaxe was driven out of Northumbria.

The next chapter will take a closer look at how the Danelaw fell.

Chapter Six: Edward and Æthelstan

Any period of sustained peace gave the Anglo-Saxons the opportunity to consolidate their positions and plan future ways of expansion into the territory of the Danelaw. It was obvious that having a foreign power control vast portions of England was not the best foreign policy. The now-settled Vikings had their own legal system, which could not be easily reconciled with existing Anglo-Saxon law. In addition, these foreigners controlled important trade routes and resources, which could impact the economy of the south. Matters were made worse when Vikings attacked Anglo-Saxon territory, acting more like brigands than peaceful neighbors. England was, for all practical purposes, a house divided. That state of affairs could not stand for long.

Edward Ascends to Power

Edward the Elder ruled from 899 to 924. He was the son of Alfred the Great, and he intended to follow in his father's footsteps as much as possible. The reconquest of England south of the Humber was a long-term goal that he pursued.

We do not know much about Edward before he became king. Asser's *Life of King Alfred*, written in 893, says that Edward was an obedient son to Alfred and somebody who treated others with friendliness, humility, and gentleness. Edward was not an ignorant clod. He was well-educated and familiar with books.

What sources we have indicate that Edward was a fighter and a popular person in the royal family. We believe that Alfred gave Edward some degree of independent authority and that the old king appointed Edward as a sub-king of Kent. Edward appeared to be a legitimate and competent successor to his father, but he would have to earn his birthright on the battlefield.

The Æthelwold Revolt

Alfred had other male kin who could make a claim to the throne of Wessex. One of them was his nephew, Æthelwold. He was the son of Alfred's older brother, Æthelred I, and Æthelwold rebelled because he believed that he had as much of a right to the throne as Edward did.

After Edward was crowned king, Æthelwold seized Wimborne in Dorset. Edward forced him to vacate that position, and Æthelwold escaped to Northumbria. There, Danes swore allegiance to him and declared him their king. Æthelwold assembled a fleet and, in late 901, landed his force in Essex. The following year, he persuaded East Anglian Danes to unite with him and began raiding in Wiltshire and Wessex. The final confrontation between Edward and Æthelwold happened in 902 at the Battle of the Holme. Æthelwold. was killed in the fight, which ended any opposition to Edward being king of Wessex.

Æthelwold's rebellion exposed a danger to Edward and his reign. It was more than just a false claimant trying to take his throne; the support of the Danes and the Danelaw was very troubling. Edward could not rest easy with a nation on his borders that could support another rebellion at a later date. There needed to be an end to any threat to Edward's power.[63]

King of the Anglo-Saxons

Alfred the Great had declared himself king of the Anglo-Saxons, and Edward assumed that same title. That was significant in itself. Edward was not only the king of Wessex and Mercia, but he was also the king of all the Anglo-Saxons who were not living in Viking-controlled areas. Many Anglo-Saxons populated the Danelaw, so Edward could conceivably say that he had the right and even the obligation to be the lord and master of those people. His title of King of the Anglo-Saxons could justify his attacks on the Danelaw, as he could say he had the intention of annexing territories where the Anglo-Saxons were concentrated.

---

[63] Anglo-Saxons.net. (2023, August 26). *Edward the Elder*. Retrieved from Early-Medieval-England: http://www.anglo-saxons.net/hwaet/?do=get&type=person&id=EdwardtheElder.

Lady of the Mercians

Edward had a sister named Æthelflæd. She was a valuable ally of the Wessex king.

To understand her political relationship with Edward, we have to look back at the reign of Alfred the Great. Mercia had been partitioned between the Anglo-Saxons and the Danes after the Battle of Edington, with the former controlling the western portion of Mercia. That part of Mercia came under the control of Æthelred, Lord of the Mercians. He recognized Alfred as his suzerain.

An alliance between Æthelred and Alfred was formalized with the marriage of Æthelred to Alfred's oldest daughter, Æthelflæd. Æthelred was a valuable ally to Alfred and helped repel Viking attacks in the 890s. When Æthelred died in 911, Æthelflæd took her dead husband's place and ruled over the Mercian territory.

An illustration of Æthelflæd.
https://commons.wikimedia.org/wiki/File:%C3%86thelfl%C3%A6d_as_depicted_in_the_cartulary_of_Abingdon_Abbey.png

She continued Æthelred's policy of closely allying with Wessex. That relationship would prove to be pivotal when Edward began to make expansionary movements into the Danelaw.

Æthelflæd was a phenomenon in an age where burly men ruled practically everything. She was a very effective ruler in her own right. William of Malmesbury, an Anglo-Norman chronicler, was effusive in his praise for this woman. In his opinion, Æthelflæd was "a powerful accession to Edward's party, the delight of his subjects, the dread of his enemies, a woman of enlarged soul."[64]

William of Malmesbury was not the only one who appreciated Æthelflæd influence and authority. Modern historians have compared her to Elizabeth I, and her stature nearly overshadows her brother. Together, Æthelflæd and Edward were a dynamic duo that would give the rulers of the Danelaw nightmares.

Building a Bulwark

We do not know much about Edward's reign from the Battle of Holme until 906. He had a truce with the Danes that year, but it was broken, and Vikings raided along the Severn. It was clear that Edward could not trust his neighbors anymore.

Alfred the Great had created a solid defensive line, and Edward improved on it. Æthelflæd joined him in defensive constructions. She built or improved defenses in Wednesbury, Bridgenorth, Tamworth, Stafford, Warwick, Cherbury, and Runcorn. The two rulers created positions that could bolster the defenses of the south against any Danish counterattack.

Edward remained busy. He sent an army into Northumbria in 909 and seized the bones of Saint Oswald (who was king of Northumbria in the 600s) in Lincolnshire. The Danes in Northumbria retaliated with a raid on Mercia. The Vikings were met by an Anglo-Saxon army at the Battle of Tettenhall, where they were defeated. After Tettenhall, the Northumbrian Danes did not go south of the Humber Estuary again, allowing Edward to concentrate on East Anglia and the Five Boroughs.

What is interesting about what happened in those few years is that Edward was encouraging Anglo-Saxons to purchase land in Danish territory. This was likely a move to solidify his claim to the territory since more Anglo-Saxons were living in Danish territory.

Another development was in combat. In the preceding years, it was not customary for Anglo-Saxons to wage aggressive, offensive campaigns. Instead, they relied on Danegeld to keep the Vikings happy and at a distance. Edward used Danegeld on occasion, but he became more

---

[64] "Order of Medieval Women." https://www.medievalwomen.org/acligthelflacligdnbsplady-of-the-mercians.html

aggressive as the years passed. He neutralized the Northumbrian Danes, which was a significant victory all by itself. Viking invasions were not as successful as they used to be.

An illustration of Edward the Elder.
https://commons.wikimedia.org/wiki/File:Edward_the_Elder_-_MS_Royal_14_B_VI.jpg

Æthelflæd went on the offensive as well. An army she sent in 917 to Derby resulted in her taking control of a significant borough of the Danelaw. This is considered her greatest triumph. The year 917 is also the year in which East Anglian Danes submitted to Edward.

Æthelflæd took control of Leicester in 918 and received the submission of the local Danish army. The great lady died in 918, and Mercia was absorbed into Wessex.

Edward continued to build forts in places like Towcester and Maldon. His armies continued to be successful against Danish troops, even taking Nottingham. The *Anglo-Saxon Chronicle* of 918 had this to say about Edward's accomplishments: "And all of the people who had settled in Mercia, both Danish and English, submitted to him."[65]

---

[65] "Edward the Elder." http://www.anglo-

Edward had effective control of all lands south of the Humber. Northumbria continued to be contested, but Edward accomplished a great deal in a few years. The concept of England as a unified country was increasingly becoming a reality, thanks to the efforts of Edward and Æthelflæd.

Letters and the Arts

Edward was an effective warrior because he had to be one. Holding on to a crown in the Middle Ages was a 24/7 job, and he needed to be on the alert for any possible threats. This did not mean that his reign was only battles and sieges. While Edward was not as academically inclined as his father, he was schooled by the scholars at his father's court and was a knowledgeable man.

We do not know how far he pursued Alfred the Great's programs for education reform, but the written script known as Anglo-Saxon square minuscule, a form of calligraphy used in the Middle Ages that made the Latin alphabet more recognizable, has its early phases in Edward's reign. We do know that there were scholarly centers in Canterbury, Winchester, and Worcester.

The surviving large-scale embroideries made in Anglo-Saxon England go back to Edward's reign. These items were taken from the coffin of Saint Cuthbert, and they were commissioned by Edward's second wife.

Edward was also responsible for the construction of the New Minster in Winchester. It was a royal abbey Edward commissioned because he wanted a building that was much grander than the older one.

A Mighty King

Edward's success in bringing England under his control is exemplified by a passage in the *Anglo-Saxon Chronicle*:

"Then Edward went from there into the Peak District to Bakewell and ordered a borough to be built in the neighborhood and manned. And then the king of the Scots and all the people of the Scots, and Raegnald and the sons of Eadwulf and all who live in Northumbria, both English and Danish, Norsemen and others, and also the king of the Strathclyde Welsh and all the Strathclyde Welsh chose him as father and Lord."[66]

---

saxons.net/hwaet/?do=get&type=person&id=EdwardtheElder.

[66] Davidson, Michael R. (2001). "The (Non)submission of the Northern Kings in 920". In Higham, N. J.; Hill, D. H. (eds.). Edward the Elder, 899-924. Abingdon, UK: Routledge. pp. 200-211.

There has been some dispute over whether this portion of the *Anglo-Saxon Chronicle* is accurate, but there's little doubt that after twenty years of campaigns, Edward had absolute control of the land south of the Humber and had the Danes on the back foot.

King Edward the Elder died in 924 while on a campaign against the Welsh. His successor, Æthelstan, was as competent a king as his father and grandfather.

Æthelstan

Æthelstan was the son of Edward the Elder and the king's consort, Ecgwynn. Æthelstan would be a credit to his father and is considered one of the greatest kings of England.

Æthelstan carried on a tradition begun by Alfred the Great: serving as a competent king of Wessex. The reputation of this monarchy was impressive, and modern-day medieval historian Veronica Ortenberg elaborated on their status, which they even enjoyed overseas.

"Wessex kings carried an aura of power and success, which made them increasingly powerful in the 920s while most Continental houses were in military trouble and engaged in internecine warfare period. While the civil wars and Viking attacks on the Continent had spelled the end of unity of the Carolingian empire, which had already disintegrated into separate kingdoms, military success had enabled Æthelstan to triumph at home and attempt to go beyond the reputation of a great heroic dynasty of warrior kings, in order to develop a Carolingian ideology of kingship."

She goes further to claim that Æthelstan was thought of as the new Charlemagne by European rulers. The days of weak Anglo-Saxon kings were long gone.[67]

ISBN 978-0-415-21497-1.

[67] Ortenberg, Veronica (2010). "The King from Overseas: Why did Æthelstan Matter in Tenth-Century Continental Affairs?" In Rollason, David; Leyser, Conrad; Williams, Hannah (eds.). England and the Continent in the Tenth Century: Studies in Honour of Wilhelm Levison (1876-1947). Turnhout, Belgium: Brepols.

A 15th-century stained-glass window of Æthelstan.
https://commons.wikimedia.org/wiki/File:Athelstan_from_All_Souls_College_Chapel.jpg

Æthelstan's succession was contested. His half-brother, Aelfweard, laid claim to the throne, and a civil war could have occurred. Fortunately for Æthelstan, Aelfweard died a few weeks after the death of Edward the Elder. Thus, a bloody war was avoided.

Æthelstan did not take any chances as far as his crown was concerned. He banished his brother Edwin to avoid any more controversy. (Some historians believe he fled to avoid his brother's wrath.) Edwin died in a shipwreck. Æthelstan regretted having to force his brother out of the kingdom. However, it needs to be remembered that these were tough times. The Vikings in the Danelaw were still there to the north and threatened Wessex's stability. Æthelstan had an obligation not just to himself but also to his subjects to see to it that the kingdom had stable leadership. He was going to make good on his responsibilities.[68]

All or Nothing

A cache of coins from the 10th century was found near Harrogate. One coin, in particular, bore an interesting inscription: "Rex totius Britanniæ" ("King of all Britain"). It was from the time that Æthelstan was the king of Wessex, and it best describes his ultimate goal. Æthelstan wanted not to be just the king of the Anglo-Saxons. Æthelstan wished to rule all of England, and he was going to try to do so.

A devout Christian, Æthelstan was probably tired of the laissez-faire attitude that the Vikings in the Danelaw had toward religious conversion. In 926, he gave one of his sisters to Sitric of Northumbria on the condition that Sitric would convert to Christianity. Sitric agreed, but soon after the marriage, he went back to worshiping the old Norse gods. Sitric died the following year, and his cousin, Guthfrith of Ivar, tried to succeed him. That was not acceptable to Æthelstan, so he drove the other man out.[69]

The Anglo-Saxon king went further. Æthelstan captured York. The significance of that conquest cannot be overstated. It was the first time that a king of Wessex gained control of a piece of northern territory. He received the submission of the Danish people of York, which infuriated other Northumbrians, as they did not want to be controlled by a southern power.

Their outrage did not matter. On July 12th, 927, at Eamont, King Constantine II of Alba (Scotland), King Hywel Dda of Deheubarth (Wales), Ealdred of Bamburgh, and King Owain of Strathclyde (a Scottish kingdom near the River Clyde) accepted Æthelstan as their overlord. The idea of a man being king of Britain was coming closer to being a reality.

---

[68] Ross, D. (2023, August 26). *King Æthelstan*. Retrieved from Britainexpress.com: https://www.britainexpress.com/History/Æthelstan.htm.
[69] Erenow.net. (2023, August 26). *The Danelaw II*. Retrieved from Erenow.net: https://erenow.net/postclassical/thevikingsahistory/12.php.

A map of Britain and Ireland in the 10th century.
Ikonact, CC BY-SA 3.0 <https://creativecommons.org/licenses/by-sa/3.0>, via Wikimedia Commons; https://commons.wikimedia.org/wiki/File:British_Isles_10th_century.svg

Æthelstan the Lawgiver

The time of peace gave Æthelstan a chance to turn his attention to other matters. The king was particularly interested in law. The Anglo-Saxons had a long history of using legal codes, and the statutes were written in the vernacular. Æthelstan took up where Alfred the Great left off. We have a massive number of legal texts that survived from his reign.

Clerical matters were essential to Æthelstan. His tithe edict is thought to be the earliest surviving law from his reign. Æthelstan introduced codes that emphasized the importance of paying tithes to the church. He was concerned about the poor, so his law code stated the amount of money that should be given to people experiencing poverty.

Threats to the social order, particularly robbery, drew his attention. The law code that he issued at Grateley mandated harsh penalties, which included the death penalty for a person over twelve years old who was caught in the act of stealing goods worth more than eight pence. Æthelstan would later raise the minimum age of the death penalty to fifteen because he believed it was not right to kill people who were so young.

Some modern historians view Æthelstan's legislation as being too harsh, but it must be remembered that the king was dealing with a rough population. Æthelstan was committed to maintaining a social code of order, and he was strict with officials, demanding their respect for the law and expecting them to do their duties diligently.

Administration

Æthelstan worked to institute a centralized government. Charters produced during his reign show his commitment to royal control over important activities.

Æthelstan made use of councils comprised of important people to exert royal authority outside of Wessex. These assemblies served to break down obstacles to the unification of England. Historian John Maddicott believed these gatherings were the beginning of formal assemblies that proved to be "the true if unwitting founder of the English parliament."[70]

Relations with the Church

Æthelstan founded churches and gave generously to monasteries. He maintained a close relationship with the church hierarchy and appointed

---

[70] Maddicott, John (2010). The Origins of the English Parliament, 924-1327. Oxford, UK: Oxford University Press.

bishops. Those he selected were often close to him. Ælfheah and Beornstan, priests who said Mass for his household, were made bishops of Wells and Winchester, respectively.

Æthelstan liked to collect relics and was known to have an extensive collection. He donated relics and manuscripts to monasteries and was a devotee of the cult of Saint Cuthbert.

Learning

Æthelstan mimicked his grandfather in his commitment to learning and ecclesiastical scholarship. His reputation for promoting education drew scholars to his court. The court was a scholarly hub for the revival of the hermeneutic style of Latin writing. An unknown scribe whom historians have dubbed "Æthelstan A" was responsible for drafting charters. His style of writing is considered the best writing of the Anglo-Saxon tradition.

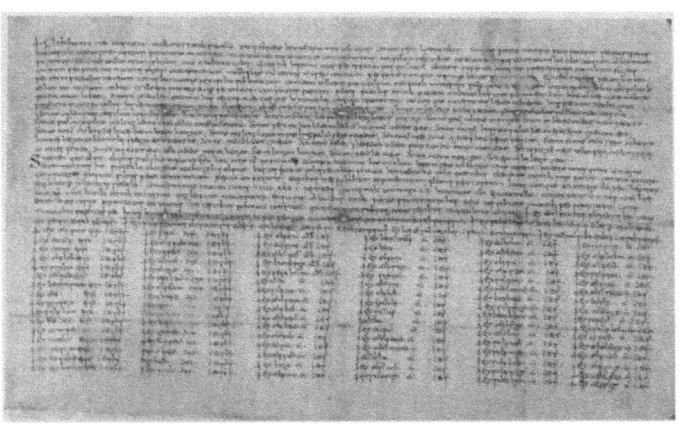

An example of the "Æthelstan A" charters.

https://commons.wikimedia.org/wiki/File:Charter_S416_written_by_%C3%86thelstan_A_in_931.jpg

Troubles in Scotland

Æthelstan had made himself the most powerful ruler in England since the Roman times, but his authority was subject to challenges. Scotland renounced its allegiance in 933, and Æthelstan had to respond. He assembled a large army at Winchester in 934 and headed north to Scotland. It was a military force that had not been seen before. Æthelstan had a mounted army and a naval force that went up the English coast and into Scottish waters up to Caithness.[71]

---

[71] Garner, T. (2018, January 2). *Michael Wood on Æthelstan's "Great War" to Unite Anglo-Saxon*

Æthelstan was able to reestablish himself, but trouble was still brewing. The Scots were not finished annoying the king.

King Constantine of Scotland forged an alliance with Olaf of Dublin, whom Æthelstan had earlier driven from York, and King Owen of Strathclyde in 937. Olaf raided Mercia, causing Æthelstan to march north with his brother, Edmund.[72]

The Battle of Brunanburh

The Battle of Brunanburh is referred to as the greatest single battle in Anglo-Saxon history before the Battle of Hastings. The site of the engagement is unknown, but the Wirral Peninsula has been suggested as the battleground. What we know about the contest is that the Celtic/Norse alliance was entrenched on the field, and Æthelstan's army mounted a cavalry charge directly at them. The *Annals of Ulster* give a description of what happened:

"A huge war, lamentable and horrible, was cruelly waged between the Saxons and the Norsemen. Many thousands of Norsemen beyond number died although King Anlaf [Olaf Guthfrithson] escaped with a few men. While a great number of the Saxons also fell on the other side, Æthelstan, king of the Saxons, was enriched by the great victor."[73]

The *Anglo-Saxon Chronicle* also recorded the battle in a long poem that includes these lines:

"Five kings lay on the field of battle, in bloom of youth, pierce with swords. So seven eke of the earls of Anlaf; and of the ship's crew unnumber'd crowds."[74]

The casualties were probably exaggerated. The outcome solidified the northern borders of England and kept the Celts in the west. The significance of the Battle of Brunanburh is that it established, without a doubt, a unified kingdom of England. Æthelstan had full control of Wessex and Mercia.

England. Retrieved from Historyanswers.co.uk: https://www.historyanswers.co.uk/history-of-war/michael-wood-on-Æthelstans-great-war-to-unite-anglo-saxon-england/.

[72] Erenow.net. *The Danelaw II.*

[73] English Monarchs. (2023, August 23). *The Battle of Brunanburh.* Retrieved from Englishmonarchs.co.uk: https://www.englishmonarchs.co.uk/brunanburh.html.

[74] English Monarchs. *The Battle of Brunanburh.*

Æthelstan died in 939 and was succeeded by his brother Edmund, who inherited the title "King of the English." Æthelstan only ruled for less than a decade, but his accomplishments were impressive. Many historians consider Æthelstan to be the father of medieval and modern England. There are those who object to this, but nearly everyone admits that Æthelstan compares favorably to Alfred the Great.

Æthelstan's reputation reached beyond the borders of his kingdom. He was held in high regard in Europe and established good connections on the Continent. Æthelstan completed the work started by his grandfather and father. His legacy as a capable warrior, administrator, and advocate for learning are well deserved.

However, the story of Anglo-Saxon England and the Vikings is not finished. Small raids were becoming rare, but it did not mean the island was safe and sound. Anglo-Saxon England was going to face a substantial threat from the northwest. Political developments in Scandinavia would eventually lead to an empire that was nearly the size of what Charlemagne ruled.

Chapter Seven: Sweyn Forkbeard and Cnut the Great

Forward to Catastrophe

Æthelstan left a strong kingdom to his successor, Edmund. The royal work of over fifty years seemed almost complete. England was a country with a strong administration, a legal code that was somewhat fair (at least for the period), and an economy that was doing great. Everything seemed to be going well for Anglo-Saxon England. However, there was a rule to be followed. Whoever was king could be one as long as he was able to protect the crown. And that was not always a guarantee.

Edmund was a young man when he assumed the throne. The former king was barely cold in his coffin when Olaf of Dublin was accepted as the king of York. He capitalized on his new title by reclaiming the Five Boroughs that had been initially taken by Edward the Elder. Olaf died a few years later, and Edmund was able to regain what had been lost.

However, his success did not guarantee that everything was going to be quiet. The king was required to put down a rebellion in Wales and was also required to deal with a troublesome situation in Scotland.

Still, Edmund was able to maintain overlordship until disaster struck. Edmund was killed in a brawl and left sons who were too young to rule. His successor was Eadred, his younger brother.

Eadred was required to deal with problems that sprang up in Northumbria. The situation was fluid, to say the least. Northumbrian magnates accepted Eadred as king but reneged on that promise and swore loyalty instead to Eric Bloodaxe. Eadred responded with a vicious raid on Northumbria. Even though he lost a battle at Castleford, Eadred was able to coerce the Northumbrians into renouncing Eric. Eadred died in 955 and was succeeded by Eadwig, the eldest son of Edmund, who died in 959.

It is important to note that the Anglo-Saxons had three kings in the span of twenty-two years. Before that, the people had three kings in sixty-eight years. The three later kings were almost constantly at war, trying to hold on to their possessions and putting down revolts. There was very little time for the stability required to nurture a peaceful society. The Anglo-Saxon kingdom that Æthelstan bequeathed to his heirs became a fairly unstable kingdom within twenty years after his death.

End of the Danelaw

Eadred did not live long enough to make a lasting impact on Anglo-Saxon history, but one very important development happened during his time on the throne. Eric Bloodaxe was driven out of York, and the people of Northumbria pledged their allegiance to the Anglo-Saxon king. The Danelaw was no more.

The Anglo-Saxons could hardly be blamed if they expressed good riddance to this northern neighbor. The Danelaw was a Viking outpost in England and a potential source of trouble. Treaties with the Anglo-Saxons were broken, and no one trusted the Norsemen on the border. The final collapse of the Danelaw would permit the Anglo-Saxon kings to have better control over the land. Surely, there would be less trouble. Or so everyone thought.

The kingdom was divided in 957, with Edgar, son of Edmund, ruling Mercia and Eadwig having suzerainty over Wessex. Edgar assumed the crown over all of England when Eadwig died in 959.

Edgar's reign differed from earlier administrations because there were no Viking raids while he ruled. His reign was viewed as a peaceful time without external threats or internal trouble. That was not to last, though.

His successor, Edward the Martyr, was murdered in 978. The man who took the next, Æthelred the Unready, would go down in history as a monarch who faced extraordinary challenges that had not been seen in Anglo-Saxon England for years.

Æthelred's reign endured raids from the Danish Vikings. These raids began in the 980s and became gradually worse. Attacks occurred all along the coastline. The brunt of the assaults was felt by the counties of

Cheshire, Thanet, Hampshire, Cornwell, Devon, and Dorset. The problems with the raids were made worse by the lords of Normandy, who permitted the marauding Danes to take refuge in their territory. Papal intervention facilitated a peace treaty in 991, but that did not stop the violence.[75]

Battle of Maldon

The Battle of Maldon would be memorialized in an Old English poem titled "The Battle of Maldon." This conflict was a disaster for the Anglo-Saxons. An army of Norwegian Vikings was confronted by East Saxons led by Ealdorman Byrhtnoth on the River Blackwater in Essex in 991. The Vikings were led by Olaf Tryggvason, who would later become king of Norway.

The Vikings were stationed on an island called Northey. There was a causeway that led to the island. The battle began when high tide covered the causeway. When the water receded, the Vikings asked to be let across to fight on the mainland. The Anglo-Saxons allowed them to do so and were defeated after their commander was killed. We will let the reader decide if the Anglo-Saxons were being polite or foolish for permitting the Vikings to cross over.[76]

The Return of Danegeld Payments

Historians note that Æthelred was often the victim of incredibly bad advice. After the defeat at Maldon, the king was advised to pay tribute to the Vikings in the hope that they would be satisfied with the cash and go away. The amount of the tribute is estimated to have been £10,000.

It appears that no one bothered to look at the history books to determine if the Vikings would actually respect those arrangements. The Vikings did not follow the terms of the agreement, and attacks continued along the coastline. London was assaulted by a large Viking fleet in 994. That fleet was a combined effort led by Olaf Tryggvason, the victor of Maldon, and Danish King Sweyn Forkbeard.

Scandinavian Nation-states

The land of the Vikings changed. It was no longer a place where clans fought blood feuds and disputes were settled with trial by combat. The

---

[75] Brain, J. (2023, August 27). *King Æthelred The Unready*. Retrieved from Historic-uk.com: https://www.historic-uk.com/HistoryUK/HistoryofEngland/Æthelred-The-Unready/.

[76] E. H. Seigfried, K. (2015, November 6). *The Battle of Maldon*. Retrieved from The Norse Mythology Blog: https://www.norsemyth.org/2015/11/the-battle-of-maldon.html.

north was becoming "civilized."

Sweyn Forkbeard was the product of the nation-state of Denmark. He was the son of Danish King Harald Bluetooth, who is credited with the conversion of Denmark to Christianity. Sweyn was not a devout Christian, but he accepted it for political reasons while tolerating the old pagan beliefs.

Sweyn was an ambitious man who made his own luck. He led a successful rebellion against his father; Harald died during the revolt. Sweyn raided London with Olaf Tryggvason but turned against his former ally a few years later and helped defeat Olaf at the Battle of Svolder in 1000. The victory allowed Sweyn to gain a portion of Norway as direct ruler and other parts of the country as a feudal overlord.[77]

Medieval Ethnic Cleansing

The raids on England continued. Hampshire, Sussex, and Dorset were pillaged in 997. Æthelred secured another truce with the Vikings for a payment of £24,000 in 1001, but this was no doubt a temporary arrangement. The king was aware the Vikings would return.

Æthelred the Unready needed to watch his back. A fifth column might have existed in the territories of the former Danelaw, whose inhabitants likely were more loyal to their blood ties than to the crown. The king received intelligence that suggested the Danes were plotting to kill him and his advisors. So, Æthelred decided to strike first. On November 13th, 1002, the king ordered the massacre of all Danish men living in the realm.

There is no record of precisely how many people were murdered. One story recorded in a charter of 1004 tells of Danish families in Oxford breaking into a church for sanctuary and the local people burning down the church and roasting the Danes inside.

Æthelred justified his actions by claiming that the decree had been issued on the advice of his leading men. If so, it was a piece of advice that had terrifying consequences.

Gunnhild, the sister of Sweyn Forkbeard, was one of the dead in Oxford. Sweyn was enraged by the news and sacked Exeter in retaliation. He went on to harass Wessex and destroy Wilton.[78]

---

[77] English History. (2023, August 27). *Sweyn Forkbeard*. Retrieved from Englishhistory.net: https://englishhistory.net/vikings/sweyn-forkbeard/.

[78] Cavendish, R. (2002, November). *The St. Brice's Day Massacre*. Retrieved from History Today:

King of England

The Viking raids intensified. Sweyn probably was no longer trying to avenge his sister's death but instead was looking for permanent control of England. He invaded England in 1013 and ultimately forced Æthelred to flee for his life. Sweyn was declared king of England but died a few weeks later, on February 3rd, 1014.

Æthelred returned from exile and drove Sweyn's followers out, but he was then forced to deal with a significant Viking invasion. Embattled and with little military support, Æthelred died on April 23rd, 1016. He lived to see Cnut, Sweyn's son, arrive in England with a massive force, but he did not live to see what Cnut accomplished.[79]

Æthelred the Unready's historical reputation has been slightly rehabilitated in recent years. In retrospect, it seems the king was a victim of circumstances that were not easy to manage, and he received some very poor advice from his counselors. His reign was the longest of all the Anglo-Saxon kings, and there were some accomplishments. Unfortunately, those are often overshadowed by his constant problems with the Danish Vikings.

An illustration of Æthelred the Unready.
https://commons.wikimedia.org/wiki/File:Ethelred_the_Unready.jpg

---

https://www.historytoday.com/archive/st-brice%E2%80%99s-day-massacre.

[79] Brain, J. *King Æthelred The Unready.*

Æthelred was succeeded by his son Edmund Ironside (also known as Edmund II), who ruled briefly. When Edmund died, the new king was someone who is considered one of the most powerful monarchs of the Middle Ages.

Cnut (Canute) the Great

Cnut was the son of Sweyn Forkbeard and was born around 990, although the exact date is unknown. Cnut would become one of the most significant rulers of the Middle Ages, as he was the king of England, Denmark, and Norway. His united realm would be known as the North Sea Empire.

Cnut was the last prominent Viking king. The age of seafaring raiders was coming to an end and would soon be replaced by nation-states with foreign policies that did not include other areas for the sake of gaining loot. Cnut was a Christian who used his religion to further his own purposes.

A drawing of King Cnut.
https://commons.wikimedia.org/wiki/File:Canute_and_%C3%86lfgifu_cropped_(Canute).jpg

He accompanied his father in 1013 when Sweyn invaded England for the last time. Sweyn's domain was divided at his death in 1014, and his other son, Harald II, became the king of Denmark. Olaf II was crowned king of Norway.

Cnut was not automatically made king of England; the English chose to restore Æthelred to the throne. That did not sit well with Cnut, who had counted on the oaths of allegiance given by Anglo-Saxon nobles. His army was too small to fight Æthelred, so Cnut sailed back to Denmark. However, before he left English waters, Cnut slaughtered the hostages who had been given to his father as pledges of loyalty. The young man was making it clear to the Anglo-Saxons that he was angry and would seek his revenge later.

Harald II was not comfortable with having Cnut in Denmark. To get his younger brother out of the way, Harald offered to support an invasion of England on the condition that Cnut would renounce any claim to the Danish throne. Cnut knew England was a bigger prize than Denmark, so he agreed to Harald's offer.

A Savage Arrival

Cnut raised an army of ten thousand men, and his strike force landed in Wessex, which he was able to subdue without much difficulty. He was supported in his invasion by Eadric Streona, the ealdorman of Mercia, who deserted Æthelred.

Cnut was out for revenge against those who had betrayed him. He moved north to Northumbria, overwhelmed it, and executed the ealdorman, Uhtred. Uhtred's death was his punishment for breaking his loyalty oath to Sweyn.

Cnut continued his war of conquest by besieging London in 1016. He soon began to deal with Æthelred's successor, Edmund Ironside. After winning the Battle of Assandun in October 1016, Cnut negotiated with Edmund.

The result was a division of England that gave Wessex to Edmund and the rest of England to Cnut. Edmund died the following January, which made Cnut the ruler of all England. Cnut celebrated his succession by executing nobles who had violated their oath of allegiance to his father and seizing the estates of other miscreants. Those lands were divided among his soldiers and other loyal followers. Cnut wanted to kill Edmund

Ironside's small children, but they were able to flee and gain asylum in Hungary.[80]

The English King

Cnut's reign of terror was over, and he got down to the business of being a monarch. He divided England into four earldoms.: Northumbria, Mercia, Wessex, and East Anglia. He married Emma, Æthelred the Unready's widow, in 1017, thereby neutralizing any challenge to his kingship that could come from the surviving children of Æthelred.[81]

Cnut did not want any more trouble in England. He recalled the Viking fleet of thirty ships in 1018 and decided to settle with the army that had followed him from Denmark. The settlement was straightforward: Cnut paid them off using the tax system that was already in place. The new king also raised £82,500 to pay the army and sent them back to Denmark. Cnut reduced his naval fleet to forty ships to bring peace and stability to the realm.

Cnut convened a council of Anglo-Saxons and Danes. An agreement was reached by which everyone was to live in peace, and Cnut would govern based on the laws and traditions that were in place before his accession.[82]

All of these actions showed that Cnut was more than a marauding pirate. He used statecraft instead of a warpath to consolidate his control over his kingdom. England was a peaceful kingdom during his reign. That was important because Cnut had a new opportunity to pursue.

Harald II died in 1018, and Cnut returned to Denmark to claim the vacant throne. He left behind a letter to the English nation, warning everyone to behave themselves in no uncertain terms:

"If anyone, ecclesiastic or layman, Dane, or Englishman, is so presumptuous as to defy God's law and my royal authority or the secular laws, and he will not make amends and desist according to the direction of

---

[80] Mingren, W. (2020, May 21). *Cnut the Great: The Myth, the Man, and the Multi-National Viking Monarch*. Retrieved from Ancient Origins: https://www.ancient-origins.net/history-famous-people/cnut-great-0013741.

[81] Parker, E. (2016, October). *Cnut: The Great Dane*. Retrieved from History Extra: https://www.historyextra.com/period/anglo-saxon/king-cnut-danish-why-called-great-rule-england-success/.

[82] Abernethy, S. (2014, January 24). *Cnut England's Danish King*. Retrieved from The Freelance History Writer: https://thefreelancehistorywriter.com/2014/01/24/cnut-englands-danish-king/.

my bishops, I do pray, and also command, Earl Thurkil, if he can, to cause the evil-dealer to do right. And if he cannot, then it is my will that with the power of us both he shall destroy him in the land, or drive him out of the land, whether he be of high or low rank. And it is my will that all the nation, ecclesiastical and lay, shall steadfastly observe Edgar's laws, which all men have chosen and sworn at Oxford."[83]

Cnut was speaking with the authority of a man who expected to be obeyed by his subjects. His previous behavior gave a good indication of what he would do if anybody tried to cross him.

Internal Politics

Cnut could be reasonably adept at royal politics. Instead of surrounding himself with Danes, he allowed Anglo-Saxons to hold important positions, such as the earldoms of Wessex and Mercia. Cnut was quick to dismiss people who were not up to his expectations. Thorkell the Tall, whom Cnut initially placed in charge of East Anglia, was outlawed in 1021.

Cnut recognized the importance of the Christian Church. He made all the outward appearances of being devout, but it must be remembered that he was a pragmatic ruler. He knew that the approval of the church would go a long way. He maintained good relations with the church hierarchy. Royal gifts to the church, including tax exemptions and grants of land, were generous. Cnut gave large gifts of money to the church, and he was a benefactor of monasteries. His actions suggest that he was able to bind the church close to him so he would not have to worry about trouble coming from the bishops.

Trip to Rome

Cnut traveled to Rome in 1027 to attend the coronation of Conrad II as the Holy Roman emperor. This allowed him to get to know Conrad and demonstrate to others that he was a pious Christian and a devoted follower of the Christian Church.

Cnut made a great impression from all accounts. He had a chance to do some favors for his subjects while he was in Rome. English pilgrims were given a reduced toll tax and were safeguarded on their way to Rome.

---

[83] Trow, M. J. (2005), *Cnut – Emperor of the North*, Stroud: Sutton.

Trouble in Scandinavia

While things were relatively quiet in England, there were some difficulties in Scandinavia that Cnut needed to sort out. He left Denmark and placed a caretaker, Ulf Jarl, in charge. Ulf Jarl was made the earl of Denmark (Ulf was also Cnut's brother-in-law).

Trouble with Sweden and Norway caused Cnut to go back to Scandinavia. He defeated the Swedes and Norwegians at the Battle of Helgeå in 1025. Cnut also had a family matter to resolve. It is believed that Ulf Jarl betrayed Cnut. Although Ulf eventually returned to support Cnut, the king did not fully forgive the betrayal. He eventually ordered Ulf's murder. Ulf Jarl was killed in a church.

Cnut moved against Norway. Olaf II had taken the throne in 1016, and Cnut wanted it back. In 1028, Cnut succeeded in driving Olaf II from his throne. Olaf's attempt to regain his throne failed. Cnut was now the king of Norway, England, and Denmark.

Master of All He Surveyed

Cnut had authority over England, Denmark, Norway, parts of Sweden, and some areas in Scotland and Ireland. He was a patron of Old Norse poetry, and his wife Emma was a patron of literature. His court was multi-national, and he had a reputation as being a wise and skillful monarch.

Cnut was also the subject of a popular legend that was recorded years later in the Historia Anglorum (*History of the English*). Cnut had to listen to a lot of flattery from the court, and he wanted to prove how empty their words were. He did so in a unique way.

Tired of being told how high and mighty he was, Cnut ordered a chair be placed on the seashore while the tide was coming in. He sat on the chair, pronounced he was overlord of the sea, and commanded the waves to stop rolling onto his land. Naturally, the waves disobeyed and kept coming in, drenching the king's legs. Cnut jumped back and declared that the power of earthly kings was empty and only God could command the waves. There are several versions of this story, but the tale shows that Cnut was smart enough to know his limitations and reminded his courtiers that their pretty words did not easily move him.

Cnut died on November 12th, 1035, in Shaftesbury. His empire quickly fell apart. Harold I (Harold Harefoot) succeeded him in England. Harthacnut took the throne in 1040, and in 1042, Edward the Confessor was crowned king.

Cnut's coronation showed the ultimate integration of Danes and Anglo-Saxons in England. The nation was no longer divided between one group and another; instead, it was a unified country. It had a tradition of law, culture, and literature, which made England stand out from the rest of Europe.

There is still one more chapter to be written about the Vikings and the Anglo-Saxons. This time, the descendants of the original sea raiders took center stage.

Chapter Eight: Stamford Bridge and Hastings

Anglo-Saxon England had a peculiar habit of canonizing barely competent monarchs. Edmund the Martyr, Edward the Martyr, and Edward the Confessor were known for leading very pious lives but having little clue about how to manage royal politics. They were holy saints at a time when Anglo-Saxon England needed pragmatic sinners. The common people would suffer from the lack of stable leadership.

Edward the Confessor was the son of Æthelred the Unready. He was born at a time when the Danes were taking the upper hand in England, and Æthelred was barely able to hold on to power. Edward was forced to flee with his mother, Emma, to Normandy after Sweyn Forkbeard took the throne. Edward spent most of his boyhood living in exile in Normandy. He had the support of many people who felt that Edward had a legitimate claim to the throne. One of his supporters was Robert I, Duke of Normandy, who went as far as to attempt an invasion to put Edward on the throne.[84]

Bloody Family Politics

When Sweyn died, Æthelred was invited to come back to rule. Edward came along with him. Æthelred died in 1016, and his son, Edmund Ironside, took over. He died later that year, and Cnut took power.

---

[84] Brain, J. (2023, August 29). *Edward the Confessor*. Retrieved from Historic-uk.com: https://www.historic-uk.com/HistoryUK/HistoryofEngland/Edward-The-Confessor/.

Edward went into exile with his siblings, but things soon became strange.

Cnut convinced Emma, Æthelred's widow, to marry him. The marriage produced Harthacnut, who became king of Denmark on Cnut's death. Harold Harefoot, the half-brother of Harthacnut, became king of England (Cnut had killed Edward's last surviving older half-brother, Eadwig). Harthacnut gathered a fleet to invade England in 1039. Emma supported Harthacnut for the throne over Edward despite Edward being her son with Æthelred the Unready. However, Harold died before the invasion could begin. Harthacnut succeeded Harold Harefoot as king of England in 1040.

This succession merry-go-round is enough to make a person dizzy. The important point is that Harthacnut was the son of Cnut, while Edward was the child of the last Anglo-Saxon king of Wessex. Harthacnut invited Edward back to England in 1041, and Edward was viewed as the eventual successor. Harthacnut died on June 8th, 1042.

The English people favored Edward to become the next monarch. In the words of the *Anglo-Saxon Chronicle*, "Before he [Harthacnut] was buried, all the people chose Edward as king in London."[85] Edward got even with his mother for her lack of support the following year. He formally stripped her of her property, and she faded from history, eventually dying in 1052.

The controversies that began with Cnut's death and ended with Edward's coronation underscore the discord and confusion that surrounded the English crown in those years. Half-brothers would take the throne and kill other half-brothers in order to keep it. There apparently was no loyalty within the royal family, and one relative would treat the other as a grave enemy. One example is what happened to Alfred, Edward's brother. He was brutally murdered by Harold Harefoot despite being a stepbrother to the king.

Godwin of Wessex

The power behind the throne for almost half of Edward the Confessor's reign was Godwin of Wessex. He played a principal role in the Machiavellian politics of 11th-century England. Cnut made Godwin the earl of Wessex in 1018. Godwin was responsible for the death of Edward's brother, Alfred, because he turned Alfred over to Harold

---

[85] Giles, J.A. (1914). *The Anglo-Saxon Chronicle*. London: G. Bell and Sonson. p. 114.

Harefoot.

What kept Godwin alive was the immense power he possessed. Wessex was a dominant earldom, and Godwin was a wealthy man. The earl's true allegiance was to himself, and though he was initially a supporter of Harthacnut, he deftly switched sides to ally with Edward the Confessor. That relationship became more robust in 1045 when Godwin's daughter, Edith, was married to King Edward.[86]

Edward chaffed under Godwin's dominance, and the tensions came to a head in 1051. Edward appointed a Norman named Robert of Jumièges as the archbishop of Canterbury. A clash in Dover prompted Edward to order Godwin, who was also the earl of Kent, to punish the town, but Godwin refused. Godwin's two sons, Sweyn and Harold, raised an army from their vassals and threatened Gloucester, where Edward was holding court. Edward's allies raised another army to counter that force. A crisis was averted when it was agreed that the meeting of the royal council, the Witan, would later convene in London.

Edward decided to press his advantage and called on all the militias of England. Godwin's own men were obliged to be part of that levy, and his sons fled to Flanders and Ireland. Edward went further in severing connections with the Godwin family by sending Edith to a nunnery.

Godwin returned in 1052 with an army. Edward was forced to restore Godwin and his sons to their estates, and Edith was restored as queen. Everything seemed to be working well for Godwin when something unexpected happened.

At a royal banquet in Winchester, Godwin denied he had anything to do with the death of Alfred, which had occurred years before. The *Anglo-Saxon Chronicle* recounts the story:

"On Easter Monday, as he was sitting with the king at a meal, he suddenly sank toward the footstool, bereft of speech, and deprived of all his strength. Then he was carried to the king's private room and they thought it was about to pass off. But it was not so. On the contrary, he continued like this without speech or strength right on to the Thursday and then departed this life."[87]

---

[86] Zimmerman, M. (2023, August 29). *Earl Godwin, The Lesser Known Kingmaker*. Retrieved from Historic-uk.com: https://www.historic-uk.com/HistoryUK/HistoryofEngland/Earl-Godwin/.

[87] Douglas, David C. (1990) William the Conqueror: The Norman Impact Upon England London: Methuen. Pg. 412.

Godwin was dead. His family was still a powerful force in England, but it did not have control over Edward the Confessor. However, Godwin's successor as earl of Wessex, Harold Godwinson, was an influential lord, and his brothers had positions of authority in England at the time of Edward the Confessor's death.

The Norman Connection

Some of the problems that Edward the Confessor had with the earl of Wessex stemmed from the growing influence of the Normans in Edward's court. Edward lived under the protection of the dukes of Normandy for years, and the English king had not forgotten this kindness. Robert of Jumièges, who was from Normandy, was an advisor to the king before he was appointed to the Archbishopric of Canterbury. Edward appointed Normans to be sheriffs in England.

We do not have a clear picture of exactly how much influence the Normans had in Edward's court. However, there is no doubt the presence of Normans was sufficient enough to make Godwin and his sons leery. The concern was well founded because the Normans would soon play a significant role in the royal succession.

The Final Years

Edward's reign after Godwin's death included vigorous campaigns against the Scots and the Welsh. However, he appeared to withdraw from active politics to go hunting. His reputation as a religiously devoted man includes the completion of Westminster Abbey, a jewel in his crown.

Even though Edward had deep religious convictions, he was still a king and had to protect his throne. He did harsh things, such as ordering the assassination of a Welsh prince. Edward's many years in exile deprived him of the ability to create a power base, so he was at odds with the earls in his realm.

A significant problem was his succession. Edward did not have any children, and he gave no clear indication of who would be his successor, which was a considerable mistake. In the opinion of historian Stephen David Baxter, Edward's "handling of the succession issue was dangerously indecisive, and continued to be one of the greatest catastrophes to which the English have ever succumbed."[88]

---

[88] Baxter, Stephen (2009). "Edward the Confessor and the Succession Question". In Mortimer, Richard (ed.). Edward the Confessor: The Man and the Legend. Woodbridge: Boydell Press.

January 5th, 1066, was the beginning of the end of Anglo-Saxon England. Edward the Confessor died that day and set in motion the events that would end with a decisive battle waged on the English southern shore. On the following day, January 6th, the Witan proclaimed Harold Godwinson to be the new king of England. He was the late king's brother-in-law. He was a very competent and powerful earl, which was sufficient enough for the Witan to make him king.

The Viking Claimant

There was a claimant to the throne in Scandinavia. The Norwegian Harald Hardrada is celebrated as the last great Viking. He was the youngest brother of King Olaf II of Norway, and he was a committed warrior.

He fought with his brother at the Battle of Stiklestad in 1030 against Cnut. Olaf was killed in the fight, and Harald barely escaped. Afterward, he became a professional mercenary and served with distinction in the Byzantine Empire and for Kievan Rus'.

Harald Hardrada returned to Norway in 1046 and wrestled the throne away from its occupant, Magnus I. Harald would spend years fighting to keep control of Denmark but failed in that effort. Harald started to look at England as a possible conquest.[89]

Harald was a distant relative of Cnut, but he had no direct blood ties to the English crown. He would have to seize England by conquest. An internal dispute improved his chances of doing that.

Tostig Godwinson was the brother of the new king of England, Harold Godwinson. Once the earl of Northumbria, Tostig was overthrown as earl by rebels who received Harold's support (Harold was convinced Tostig could not hold onto Northumbria). Tostig approached Harald with the proposal of having him take the throne of England and restoring Tostig to his earldom. Harald agreed to the idea and began assembling a fleet in the spring of 1066. He sailed from Norway after naming his son, Magnus, his successor.

The Norwegian king landed in England on September 18th, 1066, with approximately fifteen thousand soldiers. He met with Tostig, and the two

---

[89] Dr. Jessica Nelson, P. (2016, January 5). *The death of Edward the Confessor and the conflicting claims to the English Crown*. Retrieved from History.blog.gov.uk:
https://history.blog.gov.uk/2016/01/05/the-death-of-edward-the-confessor-and-the-conflicting-claims-to-the-english-crown/.

began their march south. Everything looked to be in their favor because, at the time, Harold Godwinson was anticipating an invasion from Normandy and was on the southern coast.

Harald devastated Scarborough, seized York, and won a victory at Fulford. Harald made the mistake of waiting for York to present him with hostages. He was confident that Harold could not effectively respond. Harald Hardrada was mistaken.[90]

Stamford Bridge

Amazingly, Harold led a forced march from southern England to confront the invasion force in just four days. On September 25th, 1066, Harold surprised Tostig and Harald at Stamford Bridge. The Vikings had left most of their armor behind on their ships. Harold's army charged downhill into the enemy and eventually broke the Viking shield wall.

The result was a massacre. Thousands of Vikings died as confusion took over. Both Harald and Tostig were killed in the fighting. Of the original fleet of three hundred ships, only twenty-four vessels were required to carry the surviving Vikings back to Norway. King Harold's victory was complete.[91]

Stamford Bridge was the last battle fought by the Vikings on English soil. It marked the end of Viking interest in England as a place of plunder or conquest. England was no longer part of Scandinavian politics, and its orientation would increasingly be more focused on mainland Europe. While the battle would be overshadowed by the contest that took place a few weeks later, the Battle of Stamford Bridge marks a turning point in English history.

Hastings

The main man in the 1066 drama was William of Normandy, also known at this time as William the Bastard. There is a claim that Edward the Confessor chose William to be his successor, although there is no hard evidence that this happened. William did have a connection to the English throne, though. He was the grandson of Edward's maternal uncle, Richard II of Normandy.

---

[90] Neill, C. (2023, April 17). *Who Was Harald Hardrada? The Norwegian Claimant to the English Throne in 1066.* Retrieved from Historyhit.com: https://www.historyhit.com/1066-harald-hardraada-lands-england/.

[91] Castelow, E. (2023, August 29). *The Battle of Stamford Bridge.* Retrieved from Historic-uk.com: https://www.historic-uk.com/HistoryMagazine/DestinationsUK/The-Battle-of-Stamford-Bridge/.

The Bayeux Tapestry tells the story of the Battle of Hastings. William of Normandy believed he was the rightful heir to the English throne because in 1051, or so William claimed, Edward the Confessor promised it to him.

The Bayeux Tapestry tells another story as well. Harold shipwrecked on the Norman coast in 1064 and soon after became a guest of William of Normandy. According to the Bayeux Tapestry's account, Harold swore an oath of allegiance to William and promised to support William's claim to the throne.

The Norman side of events claims that Harold was treacherous and ignored his sworn commitment, giving William the right to fight for what was his. William sailed for England on September 27th and landed at Pevensey.

Harold performed an amazing display of warcraft and leadership. Despite having already marched his men across England in a matter of days and defeating a significant enemy, Harold turned around and marched his army south.

What makes this march outstanding is the conditions under which the Anglo-Saxons moved south. The road conditions were harsher than the worst roads we travel today. It is a testimony to the professionalism of Harold's army that his troops reached London on October 6th, only eleven days after the victory at Stamford Bridge, and moved out a few days later, headed for Hastings.

The battle took place on October 14th, 1066. Despite several cavalry charges, William could not break the Anglo-Saxon shield wall and make any headway. Eventually, the Normans pulled back. The excited Anglo-Saxons gave chase, but the Normans had only been feigning a retreat. The battle turned even bloodier, and Harold was killed by an arrow hitting him in the eye. This caused the Anglo-Saxon forces to disintegrate. William, Duke of Normandy, became known as William the Conqueror. He became the king of England on Christmas Day, 1066.[92]

Interesting Theories

The engagement permanently changed the trajectory of England's history, but it was not a spur-of-the-moment decision. Events that occurred

---

[92] Augustyn, A. (2023, August 23). *Harold II*. Retrieved from Britannica.com: https://www.britannica.com/biography/Harold-II.

for decades led to William of Normandy's final choice of invasion as the only viable option. In this section, we will look at what took place regarding the succession and some things historians consider when analyzing what happened.

- The Maneuvers of Edward the Confessor

There are historians who argue that Edward the Confessor was not the simple-minded incompetent of many portrayals. He was a man who experienced the ups and downs of royal politics in the early eleventh century. Edward might have been maneuvering to protect the interests of his kingdom while he was still alive and avoid massive invasions. It is possible Edward was playing one side off against the other.

He could make promises in the dark, knowing that he would not be around to watch the outcome. The Anglo-Saxon succession was different from the rest of Europe, and Edward knew that first-hand. Primogeniture was not always the way the English crown was conferred. Alfred the Great is a classic example. The Anglo-Saxons were willing to bypass the sons of the king and permit the man who was the most capable to sit on the throne. Technically, that meant that even if Edward the Confessor made a promise to Duke William of Normandy, the king knew that the Witan could overrule his choice after his death.

Edward could make promises and assurances to both sides. He was effectively freezing them in doing that. Both Harold and William could sit back and believe he would be the king upon Edward's death. All it took was for the old king to pass away. If Edward made promises, knowing full well that the Witan could overturn the pledge, he might have done so to guarantee that his kingdom was not troubled by one party attempting to seize the throne.[93]

- Harold could have easily won at Hastings under normal conditions

There will always be debate about whether Herald made a promise to William of Normandy regarding the succession. What matters most is that Harold Godwinson was crowned king of England, and William of Normandy crossed the water to contest it. Who would have won? Encounter at Hastings. Under normal conditions? We say it would have been Harold, hands down. Here is why.

---

[93] Dr. Jessica Nelson, P. *The death of Edward the Confessor and the conflicting claims to the English Crown.*

Anyone who has read the history of the Pacific Theater of World War II can appreciate that amphibious landings are very difficult, especially when contested. The American Marines found out about that at Tarawa and Saipan, among other assaults. William would have had a difficult time succeeding if his fleet had been met on the beach by Harold's waiting army. That the Anglo-Saxons loyal to Harold could march over one hundred miles to Stamford Bridge in three days strongly indicates how tough those men were (they repeated that forced march in going from Stamford Bridge back down to Hastings.).

Harald Hardrada was one of the best military leaders of the eleventh century, and he led a force of seasoned veterans. Harold was able to surprise him and beat him. The morale of Harold's army was likely very high after defeating Hardrada. Williams's invading force was approximately the same size as Hardrada's army, so Harold's men knew they could confront the Normans without worrying too much.

The stronghold of Harold's support was Wessex. And that is where William landed. The people of Wessex would have united around Harold and put up a stubborn resistance. It is essential to remember that England had endured the invasion of Sweyn Forkbeard and other seaborne forces within living memory. They knew from either first-hand experience or the stories handed down to them by grandparents and parents what to expect and how to fight back.

William successfully landed on the beach at Pevensey and fought Harold at Hastings. The Normans were still at a disadvantage during the fighting. The Anglo-Saxon shield wall was a knight killer. William could spend the entire day sending his mounted troops against that wall, and if it did not break, all he would gain were the dead bodies of his own men. Harold could wait the entire day and, at nightfall, command an orderly retreat. William could then be drawn into the countryside to a battlefield of Harold's choosing while being harassed by Wessex partisans all the way. Harold could easily set up an ambush and destroy Williams's army.

- William desperately needed a successful diversion.

William was an illegitimate son and had to fight hard to keep his duchy. Normandy was a scene of constant fighting, and William deserves credit for keeping his enemies at bay.

England was a rich country with very fertile land. William could entice fighting men to join him in a campaign of conquest. Once he had won, William would be able to divide up the land among his winning soldiers.

That would entice men to go with him and not stay in Normandy to threaten his holdings. William needed to drain Normandy of its available manpower, and an invasion of England gave him that opportunity.

All this is speculation because the facts overrule what might have been scenarios. What we suggest is that. Edward the Confessor had reason to promise the moon to everybody, Harold had an excellent chance to win at Hastings, and William needed an invasion to secure his existing holdings.

The Days That Followed

Stories sprang up in the 12th century that Harold did not die at Hastings. It was claimed that he recovered from his wounds after two years and then went on a pilgrimage. Harold returned as an older man and lived as a hermit until he revealed his true identity before dying. It is an interesting tale, but it is the stuff of legends.

After William was anointed king of England, he introduced Norman customs to England. French became the language of the nobility, and English foreign policy became more attached to events on the Continent.

The Vikings had been a significant part of English history for over three hundred years. Their political influence died at Stamford Bridge. Even so, the Scandinavian invaders left a legacy that is still present today. But after the Battle of Hastings, it was the Normans who played a significant role in molding England. The Anglo-Saxon language and customs became less important as the years passed, as Norman became the language of the court. Then, that all changed when a royal poet named Geoffrey Chaucer sharpened his writing quill and began to draft a story in Middle English about a group of pilgrims headed to Canterbury. He helped legitimize the use of Middle English in literature.

Chapter Nine: Life of a Viking in England

The Vikings were more than robbers roaming the coasts. Many Vikings were farmers back in Scandinavia. When they were not rowing on the high seas, they were raising crops to feed their families. An increase in the population of Scandinavia caused many to look elsewhere to make a living and seek their fortune. Iceland was one destination, but a bigger one was England.

As the Scandinavians migrated to England, they settled down and made a life in their new home. We want to describe what the life of Vikings who settled in England might have looked like. We will see the day's activities through the eyes of a Viking couple named Olaf and Emma.

The Rooster Crows

It was the start of a new day. It was early spring in what is now Yorkshire, England. The sun had just come up, and the farm animals were stirring, looking for their breakfast. Olaf and Emma got up and moved about on their small farm.

Olaf was in his early thirties. There was a time when he was a crew member on a Viking longship, raiding the English coast. Those days were over. Olaf became a Christian, partly out of religious conviction and partly because he wanted to do business with Christian merchants and tradesmen. He saved enough of the money he had received from selling his loot to buy a small farm, where he made a living for himself and his family.

Emma was in her mid-twenties. She and Olaf had two children. Although life was pretty hard on the farm, she did not mind. She grew up in Norway and was used to working hard for a living.

Olaf and Emma had a small herd of sheep, two cows, and a few chickens. Olaf also had some land that grew barley and rye and pasture land where they could harvest hay and peas.

Anglo-Saxon England was a rural state, so most of the people were employed in farming. Vikings who retired from their sea adventures probably tilled their land, which they might have received for their services to their overlords. The farm would have livestock if a farmer could afford cows or pigs. Winter would have been a slow time, but the rest of the year would be devoted to raising crops. Olaf would have used the winter months to do some woodcarving, and Emma would have weaved woolen cloth.

Conversion to Christianity was not always due to religious convictions. Settled Vikings could see the advantages of becoming a Christian. It would allow them the opportunity to intermingle with other people in England and do some business. Some of the conversions were sincere, while others were not. There were situations where a Viking would convert to Christianity and still worship Odin.

Before the ground was ready for plowing, Olaf and Emma decided to make the trip to York (or Jorvik as the Vikings called the city) and sell some of the wood carvings and cloth they had produced in the dark days of December and January. Olaf approached one of his neighbors, who had a large farm, and asked if he could borrow the man's horse and wagon. The neighbor agreed, provided that Olaf would act as a sokeman and help with his harvest the following autumn. Olaf agreed.

While he conducted this business, Emma asked one of her sisters who lived close by to watch the children and tend the livestock in return for some of the money she would make in Jorvik. When Olaf returned home, he loaded the merchandise into the wagon. After dropping off the children with Emma's sister, the two headed west down a dirt road to York.

The day was pretty warm, and there was a nice breeze. Olaf and Emma took the opportunity to look around and see the sights. The territory had once been a place of violent fighting, but everything was peaceful and had been that way for several years. Their route to York was near the shore of the River Ouse. As the wagon creaked and rumbled along the path,

Emma waved at the longships that were sailing down the river toward York. These boats were loaded with trade goods that would be sold in the marketplace.

Harald Hardrada would use the River Ouse to sail up to within eight miles of York. The ability of the Viking longships to sail deep into the countryside had a significant advantage in times of peace. It meant that a city like York could benefit from maritime trade.[94]

Olaf and Emma spent the next few hours chatting and discussing what to do with the farm. Finally, just as the sun was starting to set, they glimpsed the walls of York. The city was only a few miles away.

York had everything a person needed to become wealthy and successful. It was a major market in northern England, as well as a manufacturing center. York was originally a Roman garrison town. By the 11th century, it had become an international trading hub, as evidenced by archaeological excavations of coins from Samarkand and seashells from the Persian Gulf.

How big was this city? Byrhtferth of Ramsey, writing in the year 1000, estimates the population of York was around thirty thousand inhabitants. There is, no doubt, an exaggeration. The Domesday Book suggests a population of closer to ten thousand people. That is still a substantial number, making York the second-largest city in England, trailing only London.[95] Olaf drove the wagon through the open gates of the city just before sundown. The couple was now in the largest community of people they would ever know. Being from the country, Olaf and Emma were impressed by the hustle and bustle of the city. Emma hurriedly crossed herself as they drove past an old stone church. That was not an ordinary place of worship. It was the Church of Saint Peter; it was the home church of the archbishop of York. This church was the epicenter of ecclesiastical authority in northern England.

The Archdiocese of York dates to 735 when Ecgbert, the brother of a king of Northumbria, was granted the pallium and recognized as an archbishop. The Church of Saint Peter survived the Viking invasion of 865, but it was destroyed by the Normans in 1069. The present cathedral,

---

[94] Battlefields Hub. (2023, August 31). *The Viking Invasion.* Retrieved from Battlefieldstrust.com: https://www.battlefieldstrust.com/resource-centre/viking/campainpageview.asp?pageid=541.

[95] Aitcheson, J. (2023, August 31). *York.* Retrieved from Jamesaitcheson.com: https://www.jamesaitcheson.com/england-in-1066/york/.

York Minster, was constructed between 1220 and 1472 and is considered a masterpiece of Gothic-style architecture.[96]

It was starting to get dark, and the couple needed to find a place to stay for the night. Emma was nervous because she was afraid that robbers might steal everything they had. Her fear came from the stories she had heard about the people in York. She was told they look nice but not to trust them!

Olaf told her not to worry. He had some friends from his roving days living in York, and they had invited them to stay at their house. Olaf remembered the directions and steered the wagon down the street until he reached their destination. His friends welcomed him and helped take all the merchandise into the house.

Exhausted from the trip, Olaf and Emma fell asleep quickly. The morning would be very busy. They hoped they would have a profitable day.

Off to Market!

Olaf woke up just before sunrise. He moved quietly so that he did not disturb Emma and carefully unpacked the products they wanted to sell that day. Olaf planned to sell what he made in the morning and then return to the market and sell Emma's weaving in the afternoon. He was proud of his wood carvings and had every right to be.

Viking wood carvings are a form of art. They were originally used to decorate houses, boats, and other places. It was the type of work Scandinavians would do during the long winters to while away the hours. The intricate patterns and styles are still used today and taught to enthusiastic hobbyists.[97]

Olaf was equally proud of the work that his wife did. Weaving was very important in English history at that time. Cloth-making was a skill that required patience and dexterity. Various tools, such as the drop spindle, were used to make the yarn and weave the material. Often, those tools were made from wood, bone, or bronze. Natural dyes were used to color the cloth. The process was time-consuming and required skill. Proficient weavers would produce wall hangings with the soumak technique. Other

---

[96] History of York. (2023, August 31). *York Minster.* Retrieved from Historyofyork.org: http://www.historyofyork.org.uk/themes/york-minster.
[97] Stryi Carving Tools. (2023, August 31). *Scandinavian Carving.* Retrieved from Stryicarvingtools.com: https://stryicarvingtools.com/blogs/news/scandinavian-carving.

artisans would use Emma's material to make beautiful clothing and works of art.[98]

The York Market

The first market charter for York was drafted in 700. It specified where the market would be located and on what days it would be held. Only free men were allowed to sell goods.

Temporary stalls would be erected and taken down after the market days. So, in a very prominent place, there would be an open space for a few days, while on other days, it would be packed with tradesmen and merchants selling their wares.

Olaf did not have a stall. However, that did not matter because he was not planning to have a permanent place to sell his products. Instead, he would sell things to merchants, who would then sell them to others. The same was true for Emma's cloth.

Olaf and Emma had been to the York market before, so they knew where to go to sell their merchandise. They visited a few stalls, made some transactions, and by the end of the day, the two had made a fair amount of money for their efforts.[99]

Payment

Olaf and Emma were paid with coins for their merchandise. It is not true that business transactions were all conducted in bartering. Anglo-Saxon England used coins as early as the 7th century when Eadbald of Kent first produced them. The silver penny was a common currency. Although Vikings originally used bullion in transactions, they became more comfortable using coins as they settled deeper into the English social landscape.

Dinner in Those Days

Olaf and Emma returned to their friend's home in time for dinner. It would not be a feast like the nobility would serve, but the food would be filling.

The food was plain in those days because few people could afford to put spices in their meals. Bread was an everyday staple, and it would be

---

[98] Regia Anglorum. (2023, August 31). *Textiles*. Retrieved from Regia.org: https://regia.org/research/life/textiles.htm.

[99] History of York. (2023, August 1). *Trade in the Medieval City*. Retrieved from Historyofyork.org: http://www.historyofyork.org.uk/themes/trade-in-the-medieval-city.

cooked in a clay oven. The diet was primarily vegetarian, and onions, turnips, cabbage, and carrots were standard items on the table. Salted fish or eels might be served. Meat, such as mutton, would be served on special occasions.

Fruit was seasonal and was available in the summertime and the fall. Water was polluted and not served at the dinner table. Instead, Olaf and Emma would wash their food down with diluted ale or cider.[100]

Going Home

Olaf and Emma set off for home the following morning. They gave their friends some of the wood carvings and cloth that did not sell. Going home would not take too much time because the wagon was lighter.

Olaf shared with Emma a conversation he had in York with an old friend. Leif was a former crewmate, and he and Olaf had been on several voyages. Leif did not settle down to become a farmer or tradesman. He decided to remain a warrior and was a mercenary. He shared tales of the time he spent in Byzantium as a member of the Varangian Guard.

The Varangian Guard was primarily composed of Norsemen. They were the bodyguards of the Byzantine emperor. Leif spoke of the marvels he saw of the palace and the imperial court in Constantinople. Leif also spent some time in Novgorod, where he protected merchants. Olaf enjoyed the stories but was happy with the life he was leading. His days on the water were in the past.

The Thing

Emma and Olaf were halfway home when they came upon a friend they had not seen for a while. They decided to stop and have a chat with him. The conversation went here and there. Some of the topics were items that had been discussed at the annual thing.

The thing was a Norse tradition. It was a gathering that took place annually and was a central governing body. It was a place where issues could be discussed and legal matters could be decided. Disputes could be peaceably settled. Malefactors could be tried for their alleged crimes. Fines were often levied on those found guilty.

The fine was known as wergild, which is Old English for "man payment." It was the compensation paid by the guilty party to the injured

---

[100] Roller, S. (2023, June 5). *What Did the Anglo-Saxons Eat and Drink?* Retrieved from Historyhit.com: https://www.historyhit.com/anglo-saxon-food-and-drink/.

party or that person's family in the case of death. The social status of the guilty person determined the amount. Thus, a common person's wergild was significantly lower than what was imposed on a rich man.[101]

Olaf winced as he recalled a trial at the thing. Vikings enjoyed hearing legal arguments, and trials were common whenever thing was convened. They would have twelve hereditary lawmen who would listen to cases, and freedmen were formed into committees during the court sessions. These were the origins of the jury system in Anglo-Saxon England. Æthelred the Unready helped to advance the concept of trial by jury with a legal code stipulating that twelve leading thegns (minor nobles) of each wapentake would investigate crimes without bias. Henry II would later formalize this process into the jury system.

Emma chuckled at Olaf's comments. She, too, had witnessed that trial, and it had a special meaning for her. It involved a woman who had a complaint about how a man was trying to take over her property. Viking women had rights that were unheard of in other parts of Europe. They could own property, and they could inherit their parent's estate. Viking women were permitted to make their own choices, which included their marriage partners and possessions. They could hold positions of power and authority in the community.

The couple said goodbye to their neighbor and drove on. They passed several people on the trail, and Emma noticed something that was making her feel uncomfortable. Vikings and Anglo-Saxons usually got along together, but Emma saw many frowns on the faces of the people passing by. She mentioned her concerns to her husband, and Olaf nodded his head solemnly.

The Danelaw was no more and had been gone for years. Still, people remembered the days when raids into Wessex brought about the Danelaw, and those memories died hard. Some priests were skeptical of Viking conversions and suspected that people were still practicing pagan rights in the dark.

Olaf remembered the conversations he had with a friend at the thing. King Æthelred the Unready was worried about the loyalty of the Danes in his kingdom. The ruler was starting to wonder if they were traitors. The Anglo-Saxons all appeared to worry that former Vikings wanted to return

---

[101] Nolen, J. L. (2023, August 31). *Wergild*. Retrieved from Britannica.com: https://www.britannica.com/topic/wergild.

to the days when they had significant power. Olaf was deeply concerned that troubled times were coming. He did not repeat that conversation to his wife and tried to calm her down. Still, he was worried.

They finally reached their relative's house and gathered up their children. Emma's sister drove the wagon, and the family sat in the back as passengers. Once they got back to their farm, Emma and the children went inside the house. Olaf walked over to a small shed where he kept his tools.

Once inside the shack, Olaf looked around, trying to find something. Finally, he saw a piece of Emma's cloth wrapped around something. He picked up the bundle and took off the weavings to expose its contents. It was his old battle ax. When he stopped his sea-roving days, Olaf did not leave his tools behind. The battle ax looked a little dull, but it could be sharpened until the weapon was once again deadly.

Olaf looked around the shed. In a corner, behind some farm tools, was his old shield. That was still usable. He chewed on his lower lip as dark thoughts came through his mind.

Leif had tried to persuade him to become a mercenary in Rus', but Olaf had declined. He was happy with his new life, but he was not pleased with the way things were going. His Anglo-Saxon neighbors were starting to act hostile to him. It would not take much for King Æthelred to turn on his Danish subjects. Some people would be willing to do the king's dirty work. Olaf did not like to think of it, but if anyone tried to harm his family, that fool would find out there was still some of the old berserker lurking inside him, waiting to break free.

Olaf would allow no one to destroy what he and Emma had worked so hard to create. He looked down at the floor of the shed, looking for something else. It was a whetstone. Silently, he applied the whetstone to the blade of his battle ax, sharpening the weapon until it was battle-ready.

Conclusion

The Viking era lasted a little over three hundred years, but significant changes to England occurred. The country went from four kingdoms to one unified state. That is a considerable accomplishment when one compares England with the rest of medieval Europe. Countries such as France or Spain would not be united until centuries later.

There are many components to the Vikings' story. When reading about the Vikings, it is essential to remember that some of the early accounts were written by men who had no reason to cast the Norsemen in a favorable light. Modern research and archaeology have given us a better picture of those who lived in medieval Scandinavia. The times were rough, but people were not savages. They were something far different.

England, as a nation, made substantial strides. It was a nation of laws when William the Conqueror set foot on the shore near Hastings. Charters and law codes replaced traditions and rituals as instruments of administration and justice. The Vikings have a right to claim some of these developments with the innovations they introduced.

We are not saying that the Vikings and the Anglo-Saxons turned England into an urban sprawl. However, both of them contributed to creating urban centers that did not exist before. Granted, it would be centuries before England lost its rural composition. However, the burghs and boroughs brought the benefits of urban settings and relatively large populations to England.

Norse mythology has enriched English literature for thousands of years. We still read works that Viking stories have influenced in the books of. J.

R. R. Tolkien and Neil Gaiman. Cable network programs like *Game of Thrones* and *Vikings* are full of references to legends that originated in Scandinavia.

Geoffrey Chaucer wrote in a language that had become a potpourri of phrases and words gleaned from various groups that came to England. A rich language was created with a linguistic base in Old English, French, and Norse. Many of us speak without noticing the origins of nouns, pronouns, adjectives, verbs, and adverbs. The Vikings contributed significantly to our modern vocabulary.

Viking artwork evolved over the centuries, and the influence of Viking designs has appeared in English artwork. Viking art can still be seen in various designs today, from jewelry to graphic design, especially computer games.

This is just a taste of how the Vikings influenced England. Needless to say, the Viking era was a formative period. Modern society has foundations produced by two cultures coming together. In a way, the diversity of the English society strengthened the nation, as it birthed a culture reflecting a willingness to learn rather than resist outside influences. A tradition of assimilation, not segregation, is an enduring legacy from this time.

If you enjoyed this book, a review on Amazon would be greatly appreciated because it would mean a lot to hear from you.

To leave a review:
1. Open your camera app.
2. Point your mobile device at the QR code.
3. The review page will appear in your web browser.

Thanks for your support!

Here's another book by Enthralling History that you might like

Free limited time bonus

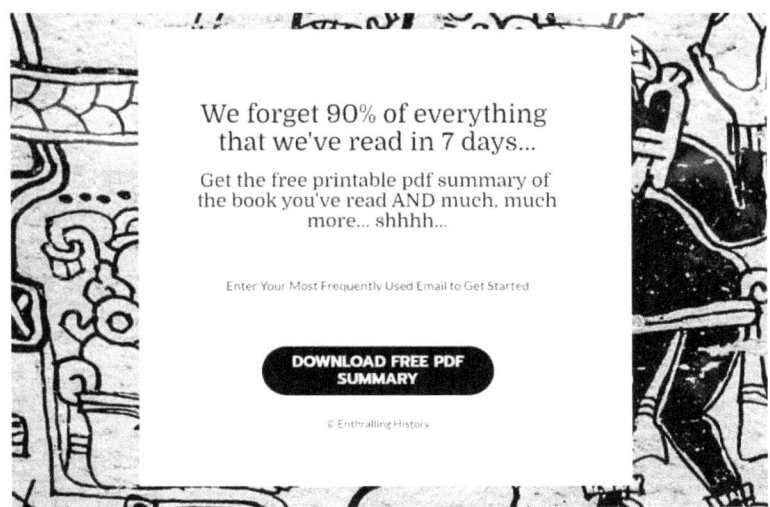

Stop for a moment. We have a free bonus set up for you. The problem is this: we forget 90% of everything that we read after 7 days. Crazy fact, right? Here's the solution: we've created a printable, 1-page pdf summary for this book that you're reading now. All you have to do to get your free pdf summary is to go to the following website: https://livetolearn.lpages.co/enthrallinghistory/

Or, Scan the QR code!

Once you do, it will be intuitive. Enjoy, and thank you!

Bibliography

The Book of Viking Myths: From the Voyages of Leif Erickson to the Deeds of Odin, the Storied History and Folklore of the Vikings
Peter Archer (Adams Media, 2017)

The Vikings
René Chartrand (Osprey, 2016)

The Penguin Book of Norse Myths: Gods of the Vikings
Kevin Crossley-Holland (Penguin, 1996)

In the Days of Giants: The Book of Norse Myths—The Beginning
Abbie Farwell Brown (e-artnow, 2019)

Norse Mythology
Neil Gaiman (Bloomsbury, 2017)

The History of the Danes
Saxo Grammaticus (Translated by Peter Fisher and edited by Hilda Ellis Davidson, 1979)

Myths of the Norse Men from the Eddas and Sagas
H A Guerber (Obscure Press, 2010)

Mythology: Timeless Tales of Gods and Heroes
Edith Hamilton (Little, Brown and Company, 1942)

Norse Mythology: A Guide to Gods, Heroes, Rituals, and Beliefs
John Lindow (Oxford University Press, 2002)

Norse Mythology: Tales of the Gods, Sagas and Heroes
Mary Litchfield (Arcturus, 2018)

Teutonic Myth and Legend—An Introduction to the Eddas and Sagas, Beowulf, the Nibelungenlied, etc
Donald MacKenzie (Obscure Press, 2010)

The Elder Edda: A Book of Viking Lore
Andy Orchard (Penguin Classics, 2011)

Tales of the Norse Gods and Heroes
Barbara Leonie Picard (Oxford University Press, 1970)

The Children of Ash and Elm: A History of the Vikings
Neil Price (Penguin, 2022)

The Poetic Edda (Translated by Carolyne Larrington)
Snorri Sturluson (Oxford University Press, 2014)

The Prose Edda—Tales from Norse Mythology (Translated by Jesse Byock)
Snorri Sturluson (Penguin Classics, 2005)

Volume 2 of Symeonis monachi Opera omnia
Symeon of Durham. Edited by Thomas Arnold (Oxford University Press, 1965)

Abernethy, S. (2014, January 24). *Cnut England's Danish King*. Retrieved from The Freelance History Writer: https://thefreelancehistorywriter.com/2014/01/24/cnut-englands-danish-king/.

Aitcheson, J. (2023, August 31). *York*. Retrieved from Jamesaitcheson.com: https://www.jamesaitcheson.com/england-in-1066/york/.

Anglo-Saxon.net. (2023, August 21). *Early-Medieval-England.net Timeline: 871-899*. Retrieved from Anglo-Saxon.net: http://www.anglo-saxons.net/hwaet/?do=seek&query=871-899.

Anglo-Saxons.net. (2023, August 26). *Edward the Elder*. Retrieved from Early-Medieval-England: http://www.anglo-saxons.net/hwaet/?do=get&type=person&id=EdwardtheElder.

Augustyn, A. (2023, August 23). *Harold II*. Retrieved from Britannica.com: https://www.britannica.com/biography/Harold-II.

Battlefields Hub. (2023, August 31). *The Viking Invasion*. Retrieved from Battlefieldstrust.com: https://www.battlefieldstrust.com/resource-centre/viking/campainpageview.asp?pageid=541.

Baxter, Stephen (2009). "Edward the Confessor and the Succession Question". In Mortimer, Richard (ed.). Edward the Confessor: The Man and the Legend. Woodbridge: Boydell Press.

Bishop, C. (2021, March 18). *Horses in battle at the time of Alfred the Great*. Retrieved from Historiamag.com:

https://www.historiamag.com/horses-in-battle-at-the-time-of-alfred-the-great/#:~:text=King%20Edmund%20of%20East%20Anglia,of%20the%20horses%20they%20needed.

Brain, J. (2023, August 29). *Edward the Confessor.* Retrieved from Historic-uk.com: https://www.historic-uk.com/HistoryUK/HistoryofEngland/Edward-The-Confessor/.

Brain, J. (2023, August 27). *King Æthelred The Unready.* Retrieved from Historic-uk.com: https://www.historic-uk.com/HistoryUK/HistoryofEngland/Æthelred-The-Unready/.

Brain, J. (2023, August 26). *The Five Boroughs of Danelaw.* Retrieved from Historic-uk.com: https://www.historic-uk.com/HistoryUK/HistoryofEngland/The-Five-Boroughs-Of-Danelaw/.

Britain Express. (2023, August 20). *Viking York.* Retrieved from Britainexpress.com: https://www.britainexpress.com/cities/york/viking.htm.

Butler, J. (2023, August 29). *The Real Ragnar Lothbrok.* Retrieved from Historic-uk.com: https://www.historic-uk.com/HistoryUK/HistoryofEngland/Ragnar-Lothbrok/#:~:text=This%20may%20well%20have%20been,settlement%20not%20far%20from%20Dublin.

Castelow, E. (2023, August 29). *The Battle of Stamford Bridge.* Retrieved from Historic-uk.com: https://www.historic-uk.com/HistoryMagazine/DestinationsUK/The-Battle-of-Stamford-Bridge/.

Cavendish, R. (2002, November). *The St. Brice's Day Massacre.* Retrieved from History Today: https://www.historytoday.com/archive/st-brice%E2%80%99s-day-massacre.

Cerdic. (2023, August 21). *Treaty Of Wedmore 878-890.* Retrieved from The History of England: https://thehistoryofengland.co.uk/resource/treaty-of-wedmore-878-890/

Chakra, H. (2021, September 27). *The Story of Danelaw.* Retrieved from About-history.com: https://about-history.com/the-story-of-danelaw/.

Curry, A. (2017). *How to Fight Like a Viking.* Retrieved from Nationalgeographic.com: https://www.nationalgeographic.com/history/article/vikings-fight-warfare-battle-weapons.

Davidson, Michael R. (2001). "The (Non)submission of the Northern Kings in 920." In Higham, N. J.; Hill, D. H. (eds.). Edward the Elder, 899–924. Abingdon, UK: Routledge. pp. 200–211.

Discover Middle Ages. (2023, August 31). *Viking Ships.* Retrieved from Discovermiddleages.co.uk: https://www.discovermiddleages.co.uk/medieval-life/viking-ships/.

Discovery. (2023, May 3). *Who was King Burgred of Mercia and what did he do?* Retrieved from Discoveryuk.com: https://www.discoveryuk.com/monarchs-and-rulers/who-was-king-burgred-of-mercia-and-what-did-he-do/.

Dorothy Whitlock, W. A. (2023, August 10). *The Period of the Scandinavian Invasions.* Retrieved from Britannica.com: https://www.britannica.com/place/United-Kingdom/The-church-and-the-monastic-revival.

Dr. Jessica Nelson, P. (2016, January 5). *The death of Edward the Confessor and the conflicting claims to the English Crown.* Retrieved from History.blog.gov.uk: https://history.blog.gov.uk/2016/01/05/the-death-of-edward-the-confessor-and-the-conflicting-claims-to-the-english-crown/.

Douglas, David C. (1990). *William the Conqueror: The Norman Impact Upon England.* London: Methuen.

"Edward the Elder." http://www.anglo-saxons.net/hwaet/?do=get&type=person&id=EdwardtheElder.

E. H. Seigfried, K. (2015, November 6). *The Battle of Maldon.* Retrieved from The Norse Mythology Blog: https://www.norsemyth.org/2015/11/the-battle-of-maldon.html.

England's North East. (203, August 10). *Northumbria's Downfall.* Retrieved from Englandsnortheast.co.uk: https://englandsnortheast.co.uk/northumbria-anarchy/.

English Heritage. (2023, August 10). *Early Christianity in Anglo-Saxon Northumbria.* Retrieved from English-heritage.org.uk: https://www.english-heritage.org.uk/visit/places/lindisfarne-priory/History/.

English History. (2023, August 27). *Sweyn Forkbeard.* Retrieved from Englishhistory.net: https://englishhistory.net/vikings/sweyn-forkbeard/.

English Monarchs. (2023, August 20). *The Danelaw.* Retrieved from Englishmonarchs.com: https://www.englishmonarchs.co.uk/vikings_11.html

English Monarchs. (2023, August 23). *The Battle of Brunanburh.* Retrieved from Englishmonarchs.co.uk: https://www.englishmonarchs.co.uk/brunanburh.html.

Erenow.net. (2023, August 26). *The Danelaw II.* Retrieved from Erenow.net: https://erenow.net/postclassical/thevikingsahistory/12.php.

European Royal History. (2022, October 22). *October 26, 899: Death of Alfred the Great, King of the Anglo-Saxons.* Retrieved from Europeanroyalhistory.com: https://europeanroyalhistory.wordpress.com/?s=Alfred+the+Great&search=Go.

Fi, B. a. (2015, May 2). *Vikings in the Danelaw.* Retrieved from Babiafi.co.uk: https://www.babiafi.co.uk/2015/05/vikings-in-danelaw.html.

Garner, T. (2018, January 2). *Michael Wood on Æthelstan's "Great War" to Unite Anglo-Saxon England.* Retrieved from Historyanswers.co.uk: https://www.historyanswers.co.uk/history-of-war/michael-wood-on-Æthelstans-great-war-to-unite-anglo-saxon-england/.

Giles, J.A. (1914). *The Anglo-Saxon Chronicle.* London: G. Bell and Sonson.

Henriques, M. (2023, July 25). *The Enduring Influence of Norse Mythology on Contemporary Culture.* Retrieved from Medium.com: https://medium.com/new-earth-consciousness/the-enduring-influence-of-norse-mythology-on-contemporary-culture-2e32cd2e3489

History of York. (2023, August 1). *Trade in the Medieval City.* Retrieved from Historyofyork.org: http://www.historyofyork.org.uk/themes/trade-in-the-medieval-city.

History of York. (2023, August 31). *York Minster.* Retrieved from Historyofyork.org: http://www.historyofyork.org.uk/themes/york-minster.

History-maps.com. (2023, August 10). *Viking Invasions of England.* Retrieved from History-maps.com: https://history-maps.com/story/Viking-Invasions-of-England.

Irvine, A. (2022, December). *10 Facts About Viking Warrior Ragnar Lodbrok.* Retrieved from Historyhit.com: https://www.historyhit.com/facts-about-viking-ragnar-lodbrok/.

Kruljac, I. (2022, August 20). *The Great Heathen Army: What was it, and how did it unite the Vikings?* Retrieved from Thevikingherald.com: https://thevikingherald.com/article/the-great-heathen-army-what-was-it-and-how-did-it-unite-the-vikings/76.

Legends and Chronicles. (2023, August 20). *Viking Children.* Retrieved from legendsandchronicles.com: https://www.legendsandchronicles.com/ancient-civilizations/the-vikings/viking-children/.

Lewis, R. (2023, August 20). *Ivar the Boneless.* Retrieved from Brittanica.com: https://www.britannica.com/biography/Ivar-the-Boneless.

MacNeil, R. (2019, May). *The Great Heathen Failure: Why the Great Heathen Army Failed to Conquer the Whole of Anglo-Saxon England.* Retrieved from Digitalcommons.winthrop.edu: https://digitalcommons.winthrop.edu/cgi/viewcontent.cgi?article=1105&context=graduatetheses.

Maddicott, John (2010). The Origins of the English Parliament, 924–1327. Oxford, UK: Oxford University Press.

Marsh, A. (2022, June 21). *In 793 AD, Vikings attacked Lindisfarne. Here's why it was so shocking.* Retrieved from National Geographic.co.uk: https://www.nationalgeographic.co.uk/history-and-civilisation/2022/06/in-793ad-vikings-attacked-lindisfarne-heres-why-it-was-so-shocking.

Medieval Archives. (2020, November 20). *King Edmund the Martyr Killed by the Great Heathen Army.* Retrieved from Medievalarchives.com: https://medievalarchives.com/2020/11/20/king-edmund-the-martyr-killed-by-the-great-heathen-army/.

Meyer, I. (2021, July 31). *Viking Art-The History of Norse and Viking Artwork.* Retrieved from Artincontext.org: https://artincontext.org/viking-art/

Mingren, W. (2020, May 21). *Cnut the Great: The Myth, the Man, and the Multi-National Viking Monarch.* Retrieved from Ancient Origins: https://www.ancient-origins.net/history-famous-people/cnut-great-0013741.

Neill, C. (2023, April 17). *Who Was Harald Hardrada? The Norwegian Claimant to the English Throne in 1066.* Retrieved from Historyhit.com: https://www.historyhit.com/1066-harald-hardraada-lands-england/.

New Advent. (2023, August 20). *St. Edmund the Martyr.* Retrieved from Newadvent.org: https://www.newadvent.org/cathen/05295a.htm.

Nolen, J. L. (2023, August 31). *Wergild.* Retrieved from Britannica.com: https://www.britannica.com/topic/wergild.

"Order of Medieval Women." https://www.medievalwomen.org/aeligthelflaeligdnbsplady-of-the-mercians.html.

Ortenberg, Veronica (2010). "The King from Overseas: Why did Æthelstan Matter in Tenth-Century Continental Affairs?" In Rollason, David; Leyser, Conrad; Williams, Hannah (eds.). England and the Continent in the Tenth Century: Studies in Honour of Wilhelm.

Parker, E. (2016, October). *Cnut: The Great Dane.* Retrieved from History Extra: https://www.historyextra.com/period/anglo-saxon/king-cnut-danish-why-called-great-rule-england-success/.

Pearce, S. (2023, February 16). *Where King Alfred Burnt Cakes in Athelney-King Alfred's Monument!* Retrieved from Third Eye Traveler: https://thirdeyetraveller.com/where-king-alfred-burnt-cakes-in-athelney-king-alfreds-monument/.

Regia Anglorum. (2023, August 31). *Textiles.* Retrieved from Regia.org: https://regia.org/research/life/textiles.htm.

Roller, S. (2023, June 5). *What Did the Anglo-Saxons Eat and Drink?* Retrieved from Historyhit.com: https://www.historyhit.com/anglo-saxon-food-and-drink/.

Ross, D. (2023, August 26). *King Æthelstan.* Retrieved from Britainexpress.com: https://www.britainexpress.com/History/Æthelstan.htm.

Ross, D. (2023, August 21). *The Battle of Edington.* Retrieved from Britain Express: https://www.britainexpress.com/History/battles/edington.htm.

Roua, V. (2016, May 7). *A Brief History of the Danish Vikings and of the Danelaw.* Retrieved from Thedockyards.com: https://www.thedockyards.com/the-danish-vikings-and-the-danelaw/.

Shipfans.blogspot.com. (2023, August 10). *Drakkar Viking Ship 9th-132th century.* Retrieved from Shipfans.blogspot.com: http://shipfans.blogspot.com/2010/04/drakkar-viking-ship-9th-13th-century.html

Skald, F. t. (2016, September 16). *Viking History: Post-by-Post.* Retrieved from Fjorn-the-skald.tumblr.com: https://fjorn-the-skald.tumblr.com/post/150515624715/lesson-16-viking-money-commerce-coins-and.

Skjaden. (2020, January 16). *Trade in the Viking Age-Do You Know Which Trade Towns That Were the Most Important Ones?* Retrieved from Nordic Culture: https://skjalden.com/where-did-the-vikings-trade/.

Sky History. (2023, August 20). *11 Facts About Fearsome Viking "Ivar the Boneless."* Retrieved from www.history.co.uk: https://www.history.co.uk/articles/11-facts-about-fearsome-viking-ivar-the-boneless.

Sky History. (2023, August 26). *Old Norse Words We Use Every Day.* Retrieved from www.history.co.uk: https://www.history.co.uk/shows/vikings/articles/old-norse-words-we-use-every-day.

Sky History. (2023, August 20). *Who Was Viking Legend Bjorn Ironside.* Retrieved from History.co.uk: https://www.history.co.uk/articles/who-was-viking-legend-bjorn-ironside

Stryi Carving Tools. (2023, August 31). *Scandinavian Carving.* Retrieved from Stryicarvingtools.com: https://stryicarvingtools.com/blogs/news/scandinavian-carving.

The History Junkie. (2023, August 21). *5 Reasons That Burhs Were Important and How They Helped Alfred the Great Defeat the Vikings.* Retrieved from Thehistoryjunkie.com: https://thehistoryjunkie.com/5-reasons-that-burhs-were-important-and-how-they-helped-alfred-the-great-defeat-the-vikings/.

The Ministry of History. (2020, May 5). *Ragnar Lothbrok.* Retrieved from Theministryofhistory.co.uk: https://www.theministryofhistory.co.uk/historical-biographies/ragnarlothbrok.

The Viking Answer Lady. (2023, August 29). *Origin of the phrase, "A furore Normannorum libera nos, Domine.* Retrieved from The Viking Answer Lady: http://www.vikinganswerlady.com/vikfury.shtml.

Thomsen, M. H. (2023, August 10). *Instrument navigation in the Viking Age?* Retrieved from Vikingeskibs Muskeet: https://www.vikingeskibsmuseet.dk/en/professions/education/knowledge-of-sailing/instrument-navigation-in-the-viking-age.

Trow, M. J. (2005), *Cnut – Emperor of the North*, Stroud: Sutton.

Ulvog, J. (2017, November 8). *Size of Viking raiding parties.* Retrieved from Ancientfinances.com: https://ancientfinances.com/2017/11/08/size-of-viking-raiding-parties/#:~:text=In%20The%20Vikings%20course%20from,500%20up%20to%201%2C200%20warriors.

Viking.no. (2004, August 14). *The Danelaw: Population, culture and heritage.* Retrieved from Viking.no: https://www.viking.no/e/england/danelaw/e-heritage-danelaw.htm.

Viking.no. (2004, August 14). *Trade routes in the British Isles.* Retrieved from Viking.no: https://www.viking.no/e/england/york/jorvik_trading_centre_2.html.

Warriors & Legends. (2023, August 20). *Viking Warrior Raids.* Retrieved from Warriorsandlegends.com: https://www.warriorsandlegends.com/viking-warriors/viking-warrior-raids/.

Warriors and Legends.com. (2023, August 31). *Famous Viking Warriors.* Retrieved from Warriorsandlegends.com: https://www.warriorsandlegends.com/viking-warriors/famous-viking-warriors/.

Williamson, J. (2022, August 20). *Who was Ubba Ragnarsson, the Viking commander of the Great Heathen Army?* Retrieved from Thevikingherald.com: https://thevikingherald.com/article/who-was-ubba-ragnarsson-the-viking-commander-of-the-great-heathen-army/194.

Zimmerman, M. (2023, August 29). *Earl Godwin, The Lesser Known Kingmaker.* Retrieved from Historic-uk.com: https://www.historic-uk.com/HistoryUK/HistoryofEngland/Earl-Godwin/.

www.ingramcontent.com/pod-product-compliance
Lightning Source LLC
Chambersburg PA
CBHW070328010526
44107CB00004B/453